ANA'S CITY GUIDE
TOKYO

Tokyo:Yesterday and Tomorrow

The world's major cities are filled with contrasts but none revels in the juxtaposition of tradition and novelty as does Tokyo. Gleaming intelligent buildings bristle with cutting-edge technology. But just around the corner are stately temples crafted by ages-old wooden building techniques. Modern superhighways soar over narrow twisting alleys laid out centuries ago. The most advanced electronics are just a few shelves away from traditional handicrafts. Tokyo maintains its ties to the past even as it creates the ideal city of tomorrow.

City of Tradition

The old Tokyo lives on in such time-honored institutions as the Kabuki-za Theater and Sensoji Temple. In some cases, tradition is best served by new facilities. The Kokugikan sumo arena, National Theater of Japan and Ota Memorial Museum of Art allow traditional sports and arts to thrive in a new age.

Ota Memorial Museum of Art

The National Theater of Japan

The Kokugikan, site of sumo tournaments

Sensoji Temple incense urn

Korakuen park's Japanese garden

Yushima Jinja Shrine

The University of Tokyo's Red Gate

The ornately decorated Kabuki-za Theater

City of People

Tokyo residents relish the blend of old and new. One glance can often catch both kimono and fashions straight from the runways of Paris and Milan. Leisure activities range from a quiet stroll under age-old cherry trees to frenzied dancing to the latest disco hits. Dining includes traditional favorites like soba, as well as new cuisine from all over the world.

The Nakamise at Sensoji Temple

Strolling under the cherry blossoms

Lunchtime in Hibiya Park

Kimono can still be seen

Harajuku street vendors

Tourists at Sensoji Temple

Trendy Shibuya

Typical Tokyo bus stop

Hibiya Park, an oasis in the center of Tokyo

City of Promise

Every Tokyo vista seems to include futuristic architecture, from small residences to sky-scrapers. State-of-the-art technology permeates such new landmarks as Tokyo Dome and Suntory Hall. These new developments are integrated into the existing city fabric as Tokyo constantly changes into the city of tomorrow.

Asahi Breweries Ltd.,'s Super Dry Hall restaurant

Ochanomizu Square

Ark Hills' Suntory Hall, site of popular and classical concerts

TEPCO Electric Energy Museum

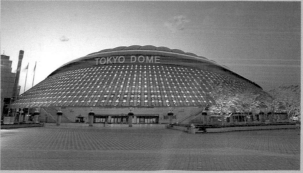

Tokyo Dome, Japan's first enclosed baseball stadium

ANA'S CITY GUIDE
TOKYO

Local area maps are from Tokyo Bilingual Atlas, produced by Iris Co., Ltd., published by Kodansha Ltd.

Photographs are from the following sources: Issei Ota, Kodansha Photo Library, PANA Tsushin, Sekai Bunka Photo, Kyodo Photo Service, and Remote Sensing Technology Center of Japan.

The section "An Introduction to Japanese Cuisine" was prepared by Lucy Seligman Kanazawa.

Distributed in the United States by Kodansha America, Inc., 114 Fifth Avenue, New York, N.Y. 10011, and in the United Kingdom and continental Europe by Kodansha Europe Ltd., 95 Aldwych, London WC2B 4JF. Published by Kodansha Publishers Ltd., 12-21 Otowa 2-chome, Bunkyo-ku, Tokyo 112.

ISBN 4-7700-1527-5

Contents

Sidebar Contents

About This Book

Tokyo, the capital and cosmopolitan metropolis of Japan, can be a city of baffling contrasts to the newcomer.

Birthplace to some of Japan's most sacred national treasures, centuries-old customs and traditions, Tokyo is also a labyrinth of concrete and steel rising up to a gray skyline, a by-product of one of the most booming economies the world has ever known.

However long or short your visit, Tokyo offers many unique experiences for the open-minded traveler. We hope that our *ANA's City Guide Tokyo* can serve the visitor by providing a guide to the sights, sounds, and tastes that are a part of this dynamic and youthful city. Besides introducing Tokyo, this book also provides brief highlights on nearby cultural attractions and several other major Japanese cities. Sidebars contain useful information as well as interesting highlights on the city that you are not likely to find in other publications. (Refer to the table of contents in each section for listings on sidebars.)

While we have supplied the latest information on prices, opening and closing times, and telephone numbers for a variety of establishments, it is always best to anticipate changes. Tokyo, after all, is a city that thrives on change.

Welcome to Tokyo

Although much of this ultra-modern city was rebuilt from the ashes of World War II, a leisurely walk almost anywhere in Tokyo is apt to lead you to a neighborhood Shinto shrine, its mossy stone walls enclosing ages of traditional culture.

Within a thirty-mile radius of Tokyo's Imperial Palace, around which the city first flourished at the beginning of the seventeenth century, live twenty-eight million people. This is more than the entire population of the state of California, and yet Tokyo boasts one of the lowest crime rates in the world.

To manage such masses, Tokyo has a convenient network of trains, subways, streetcars, and buses, tying together more than 1,000 stations in Tokyo's twenty-three wards with such precision that public transportation throughout the city's 238 square miles is relatively inexpensive and quick. This is attested to by the more than 22.5 million people who use this system daily.

For the first-time visitor, finding any place in this city of unaddressed, unmarked, and often unnamed streets requires a map, if not a detailed explanation. Yet, in spite of Tokyo's seemingly endless sprawl, the city is divided into literally hundreds of separate neighborhoods, each of which is within walking distance of a subway or train station. Each neighborhood has its own police box, with a policeman on duty whose many functions include helping those who are lost to find their way (unbelievably, the city's taxi drivers seem acquainted with every hidden corner).

Tokyo's neighborhoods, each with its own distinctive personality, are virtually towns in themselves, self-sufficient communities for living and working. We'll explore Tokyo's major neighborhoods in the following sections.

A Brief Look at Japan's History

Although Japan has been inhabited for over 100,000 years, its legendary history doesn't begin until 660 B.C., with the enthronement of the first Emperor Jimmu, whose lineage myth traces directly to the Sun Goddess, Amaterasu-o-mikami. For the next eighteen centuries Japan was ruled by the Imperial Court. With the establishment of the Kamakura Shogunate in A.D.1192, the government changed to a system of military feudalism. The Meiji Restoration of 1867 saw power restored from the Shoguns to the Emperor. A period of rapid modernization ensued, during which the administration of the country followed Western ideas and Japan took its place among the great nations. The Imperial reign which began with the enthronement of the Emperor Meiji ended with the final tragedies of World War II, from whose ashes Japan has emerged as one of the leading economic powers of the world.

The Beginning of Historical Japan

With the introduction of Buddhism and the Chinese writing system in the sixth century, Japan entered its historical phase. With it came the adoption of Chinese literature, arts, sciences, architecture, and the Chinese calendar. Prince Shotoku (572–621), considered the father of Japanese Buddhism, did much to usher in these improvements. As Imperial Regent, he supported Buddhism, and utilized Chinese and Korean culture to advance the rudimentary administration of Japan. He built great Buddhist temples, among them Horyu-ji (607) near Nara, which has the oldest surviving wooden structure in the world. The scale and grandeur of this temple testify to the power and influence Buddhism had attained in such a short period of time.

The Nara Period (710–784)

The first permanent capital was established in Nara in 710. It was during the Nara Period that Japan's two oldest historical works, the *Koji-ki* ("Record of Ancient Matters") and the *Nihon-shoki* ("Chronicles of Japan"), were compiled. The first national poetry and songs were produced, which have been handed down in an anthology of nearly 5,000 poems called the *Manyoshu* ("Collection of 10,000 Leaves"). The Fujiwara, a powerful court family, established the Buddhist Kofuku-ji temple and the Shintoist Kasugi Shrine at the new capital. The Emperor built Todai-ji temple, where the Great Buddha was housed in the world's largest wooden building, as the imported creed of Buddhism continued to flourish under the protection of the national Shintoists of the Imperial Court.

The Heian Period (794–1192)

As the powerful Buddhist priests extended their activities to become involved in politics, the Emperor removed the capital to Kyoto in 794 in order to rid the Court of their influence. This was the beginning of the Heian Period, centered in the capital at Kyoto, where extravagant court life and the arts flourished, particularly architecture. Lady Murasaki documented court life in the *Tale of Genji*, the world's first psychological novel, and Seii Shonagon compiled her collection of essays entitled *The Pillow Book*. Imperial power was consolidated under the rule of the Fujiwara family, who reigned as regents to the Emperor. The most powerful among them was Fujiwara no Michinaga (966–1027), whose son, Yorimichi, built the famous Phoenix Hall at Byodo-in temple. A reform movement in Buddhism began when two leading Buddhist priests,

Saicho and Kukai, went to study in China. The former returned to establish the Tendai sect, and built his headquarters on Mt. Hiei in Kyoto. Kukai founded the Esoteric Buddhist sect of Shingon, erecting monasteries at Kyoto's To-ji temple and on Mt. Koya.

For centuries following, Kyoto prospered under the political and economic rule of the families at court, who, along with the Buddhist priests, dominated the capital's cultural activities as well. The nobility, however, neglected the arts of war, and with the economic development of the rural areas a new class of military leaders arose. The most influential of these were the Taira family of western Japan, and the Minamoto family of the east. Imperial authority gradually waned, disorder arose, and revolts were frequent. In the late eleventh century, the Fujiwara lost control of power, and Japan was polarized around the Taira and the opposing Minamoto. The ensuing period of bloody civil war ended with the annihilation of the Taira by the Minamoto in 1185. By now, the Imperial Court had virtually lost all of its power, which, with the exception of a brief three-year period, would not be restored for nearly seven centuries.

The Kamakura Period (1192–1333)

The victorious Minamoto Yoritomo became the new ruler of Japan, marking the arrival of the samurai as the ruling class. Yoritomo assumed the title of Seii-taishogun (literally, "Commander-in-Chief of the Expeditionary Forces Against the Barbarians"), and far away from the Imperial Court at Kyoto, established Japan's first independent military government at the eastern port of Kamakura. In contrast to the Heian Period, the culture of the Kamakura Period

was war-oriented, as reflected in the arts during this period. The making of armor and swords reached new heights, and literature consisted mainly of historical narratives, such as *The Tale of the Heike*, which chronicled the fall of the Taira clan.

Ashikaga Period (1333–1573)

In 1333 the seat of power shifted back to the Imperial Court for three short years, under the Emperor Go-Daigo. In 1336 the warlord Ashikaga Takauji deposed the Emperor, created the Northern Dynasty, and established a new military regime in Kyoto that would rule for over two centuries. Go-Daigo courageously resisted, and the nearly six decades that his sons and grandsons continued the fight are called the period of the Southern and Northern Dynasties. In 1392 the Imperial schism was closed in favor of the South, and the Northern Dynasty came to an end, but the Ashikaga influence can be felt even today in the culture of flower arrangement, the tea ceremony, and *Noh* drama. Kyoto's famous Gold and Silver Pavilions were constructed during this period.

Azuchi-Momoyama Period (1573–1600)

For all their power in Kyoto, the Ashikaga were unable to dominate the rural areas for very long. From 1490, Japan was ravaged by a century of civil wars among local warlords. In the second half of the sixteenth century, Oda Nobunaga rose up to become master of several provinces. So great was Nobunaga's reputation as a military strategist that the Emperor Ogimachi invited him to reestablish order in the nation. In 1573, Nobunaga attacked Kyoto, and overthrew the Ashikaga Shogunate. Two years later he built Azuchi Castle, Japan's first important feudal castle, setting an example which was followed by hundreds of warlords by the end of the century. While on the brink of unifying the nation in 1582, Nobunaga was assassinated by one of his own vassals. One of Nobunaga's generals, Toyotomi Hideyoshi, who had risen from the peasant classes to a position of power, crushed the insurgents, and went on to complete the establishment of a centralized government. Hideyoshi built several palatial fortresses, including Fushimi Castle south of Kyoto, and the mighty Osaka Castle. He was a patron of the great tea master Sen no Rikyu, and though his de facto rule was short lived, the era of peace which began in the late sixteenth century witnessed a flourishing of the arts. The paintings of the Kano School were created during this period, as were the prototypes of modern kabuki and *bunraku* (puppet drama). After Hideyoshi's death in 1598 two of his most powerful generals, Ishida Mitsunari and Tokugawa Ieyasu, vied for power. A decisive battle between the two forces was waged at Sekigahara in 1600. Ieyasu, from the east, defeated his western enemies and established the Tokugawa Shogunate, which would rule Japan for the next two and a half centuries from the military capital at Edo (modern-day Tokyo).

Edo (Tokugawa) Period (1603–1867)

Ieyasu's immediate successors strengthened the authoritarian reign which he had imposed upon the entire nation. Christianity was banned, and with the exception of Nagasaki, all Japanese ports were closed to the outside world. Only Dutch and Chinese traders were allowed into a carefully monitored area of Nagasaki, assuring the Tokugawa a monopoly on foreign trade. To ensure the loyalty of Tokugawa allies, and to discourage would-be rivals from rebelling, the Edo government imposed the so-called system of alternate attendance in the capital. Accordingly, all feudal lords, who originally numbered over three hundred, were obligated to maintain costly residences in Edo, in addition to estates in their own domains. They were forced to travel back and forth between their home territories and the Shogun's capital, with a retinue of vassals, servants, and porters befitting their rank. This costly enterprise, conducted in alternate years, put such financial strain on all the landed barons, that an attack against the Shogunate was an economic impossibility. And as a final security measure, the law forced the wife and heir of each feudal lord to reside permanently in Edo as virtual hostages.

The isolation which lasted for over two centuries of harsh Tokugawa rule was the longest era of peace in Japanese history. Society consisted of four distinctly separate classes. The warrior class, or samurai, were the overlords of the peasants, artisans and merchants, whose social rank descended in that order. Amid the constant comings and goings of the retinues of the feudal lords, an urban middle class developed in Edo, which flourished as a center of trade to a degree unknown anywhere else in the world. By the end of the 1700s the population of Edo had grown to one million, and by the middle of the next century, with more people than the combined populations of London and Paris, Edo was the largest city in the world. Economic progress allowed even the commoners to engage in cultural activities. *Ukiyo-e* wood-block prints depicted the pleasure quarter of Yoshiwara, the bathhouses, kabuki drama, and the scenic wonders of Japan. It was during this period that the now-famous poet Basho

Ark Hills: a futuristic mini city in Akasaka

made his literary pilgrimage to the north, and that the short, stylized verse of haiku achieved great popularity. Despite the spartan code of ethics followed by the samurai, the culture of the Edoite thrived.

Modern Japan

The isolated nation was aroused from two centuries of what some historians liken to blissful slumber when Commodore Perry's flotilla of so-called Black Ships were sighted off Tokyo Bay in 1853. The foreigners demanded that Japan open its doors to the outside world, and when it became clear that the Tokugawa Shogunate was no longer able to defend the technologically backward nation from the Western onslaught, the government began to crumble. Turbulence filled the years that followed, and in 1867 the Shogun's military government came to an official end with the restoration of power to the Emperor Meiji. The Imperial capital was moved from Kyoto to Edo, which was renamed Tokyo, and the Imperial family took up residence there.

The decades following the Meiji Restoration witnessed the modernization of Japan. The feudal lords were deprived of their fiefs, and the samurai their swords. Children of all classes received compulsory education. The Imperial government aggressively adopted Western culture, technology, and political and social structures, and took measures to ensure the growth of industry. But in spite of Westernization and the democratic movements of the latter part of the nineteenth century, Japan's traditional, unequal social structure survived. The Emperor was the sovereign ruler. Only members of a newly formed aristocracy could serve in the House of Councillors, and only men who paid a certain amount of taxes were eligible to vote for members of the House of Representatives. A powerful nation was the result of rapid modernization, and less than forty years after the Meiji Restoration, Japan's victory in the Russo-Japanese War did much to dispel the myth of Western superiority over Asia. With the annexation of Korea in 1910, Japan began the active pursuit of imperialist ambitions in Asia. The annexation of Manchuria eventually led to war with the United States, during which Japan mounted one of the greatest military efforts in modern history. Defeat in World War II, and the ensuing American Occupation, brought on sweeping political and social reforms. Japan became a true democracy, and the Emperor, who during recent decades had been revered as a god, renounced his deification. Democratically elected officials ushered in social equality, while the 1964 Tokyo Olympic heralded unprecedented economic growth which continues today.

THE TOKYO
METROPOLITAN AREA
首都圏

Arriving at Narita

After disembarking at Terminal 2 of Narita's New Tokyo International Airport, pass through the quarantine station, then continue to one of the immigration counters marked "Foreign Passports." Present your passport and the completed disembarkation card (which you should have been given during the flight) to an immigration officer.

After you have passed through immigration, take one of the stairways leading down to the ground level where the baggage claim is. There the baggage monitor will show your flight number. (Luggage carts are available at no charge in the baggage claim area.) If you have any plants or animals, proceed to the quarantine counter indicated, then go to the customs counters. If you have nothing to declare, go to one with a green sign, hand your completed customs form (which you should have been given during the flight) to the officer and let him inspect your baggage.

Once you have passed through customs, you may buy Japanese yen at one of the bank-teller windows near the exit doors leading to the airport lobby.

New Tokyo International Airport (Narita)

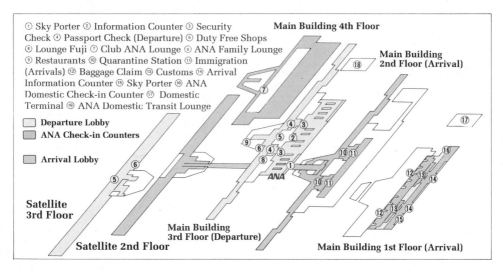

① Sky Porter ② Information Counter ③ Security Check ④ Passport Check (Departure) ⑤ Duty Free Shops ⑥ Lounge Fuji ⑦ Club ANA Lounge ⑧ ANA Family Lounge ⑨ Restaurants ⑩ Quarantine Station ⑪ Immigration (Arrivals) ⑫ Baggage Claim ⑬ Customs ⑭ Arrival Information Counter ⑮ Sky Porter ⑯ ANA Domestic Check-in Counter ⑰ Domestic Terminal ⑱ ANA Domestic Transit Lounge

Departure Lobby
ANA Check-in Counters
Arrival Lobby

Main Building 4th Floor
Main Building 2nd Floor (Arrival)
Satellite 3rd Floor
Satellite 2nd Floor
Main Building 3rd Floor (Departure)
Main Building 1st Floor (Arrival)

Point of/from Narita	Distance (km)	Time (minutes) & Fare		Bus
Haneda Airport	83.2	🚌 90 ¥2,900	🚕 80 ¥25,000	Taxi
Tokyo (JR)	79.2	🚌 53 ¥2,890	🚆 90 ¥1,260	Railway
Ueno (Keisei Line)	68.5	🚌 62 ¥1,880	🚆 75 ¥980	
Tokyo City Air Terminal	71.2	🚌 80 ¥2,700	🚕 80 ¥16,500	
Yokohama City Air Terminal	104.5	🚌 120 ¥3,300		

Note: Approximate times and fares as of June 1, 1996.

Getting In and Out of Tokyo

Access Between Narita and Tokyo

Narita Airport is forty-one miles (sixty-six kilometers) from Tokyo, and the transportation alternatives are: JR Narita Express train, Keisei Skyliner express train, limousine bus, or airport taxi.

JR Narita Express train: This runs directly to and from the airport terminal and Tokyo Station (fare: ¥2,890), Shinjuku and Ikebukuro stations (fare: ¥3,050), and Yokohama station (fare: ¥4,100). The Narita/Tokyo trip takes sixty minutes, and reservations are required.

The Keisei Skyliner express train: This leaves every forty minutes and takes sixty minutes between Narita Airport Station and Ueno Station in Tokyo (fare: ¥1,880).

Limousine buses: These leave regularly from the airport to major Tokyo hotels, and to Shinjuku, Ikebukuro, and Tokyo stations (and a few others) as well as to Tokyo City Air Terminal (TCAT), near the center of the city, and Yokohama City Air Terminal (YCAT), near Yokohama Station. Depending on your destination and traffic conditions, the trip takes anywhere from fifty-five minutes to two hours. The fare will be between ¥2,200 and ¥3,800. If the bus does not stop at your hotel, take it to the nearest major hotel and catch a cab from there. There is also a limousine bus service to Tokyo Disneyland.

Airport taxis: These are quite expensive but convenient if you are a party of three to four people or if you have a lot of luggage. The sixty- to ninety-minute taxi ride to downtown Tokyo will cost over ¥20,000 (Note that you will also have to pay the highway tolls of about ¥2,350).

Tourist Information: The two counters of this free service are on the 1st floor of Terminal 2, near the central exit. Advice is provided on getting to Tokyo and on sightseeing, and hotels can also be booked for you anywhere in Japan.

Leaving from Narita

You must arrive at least two hours before your flight departure time. Please note that there is a Passenger Service Facilities Charge for departing passengers (¥2,000 adults; ¥1,000 children; cash or JCB, Visa, Masters, Diners, and Amex credit cards). If you are flying with ANA, you may check in at Tokyo City Air Terminal (TCAT) in downtown Tokyo.

Kansai International Airport

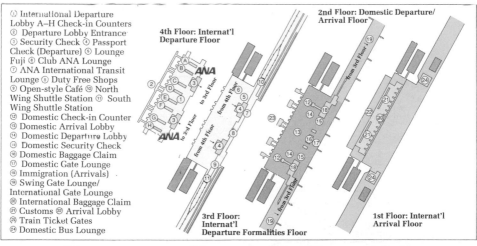

① International Departure Lobby A–H Check-in Counters ② Departure Lobby Entrance ③ Security Check ④ Passport Check (Departure) ⑤ Lounge Fuji ⑥ Club ANA Lounge ⑦ ANA International Transit Lounge ⑧ Duty Free Shops ⑨ Open-style Café ⑩ North Wing Shuttle Station ⑪ South Wing Shuttle Station ⑫ Domestic Check-in Counter ⑬ Domestic Arrival Lobby ⑭ Domestic Departure Lobby ⑮ Domestic Security Check ⑯ Domestic Baggage Claim ⑰ Domestic Gate Lounge ⑱ Immigration (Arrivals) ⑲ Swing Gate Lounge/International Gate Lounge ⑳ International Baggage Claim ㉑ Customs ㉒ Arrival Lobby ㉓ Train Ticket Gates ㉔ Domestic Bus Lounge

4th Floor: Internat'l Departure Floor

2nd Floor: Domestic Departure/Arrival Floor

3rd Floor: Internat'l Departure Formalities Floor

1st Floor: Internat'l Arrival Floor

☐ Internat'l Departure Floor   ☐ ANA Check-in Counters   ☐ Internat'l Arrival Floor

☐ Rail Stations/Car Parks/Connecting Walkways   ☐ Domestic Floor

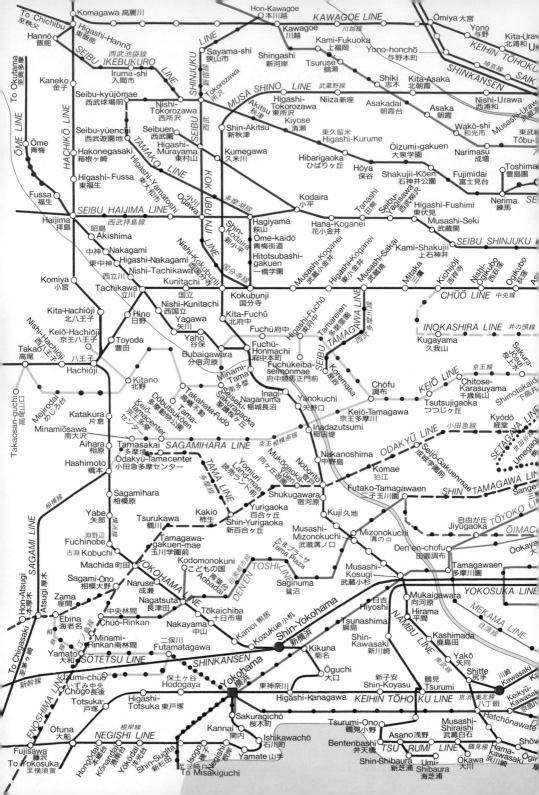

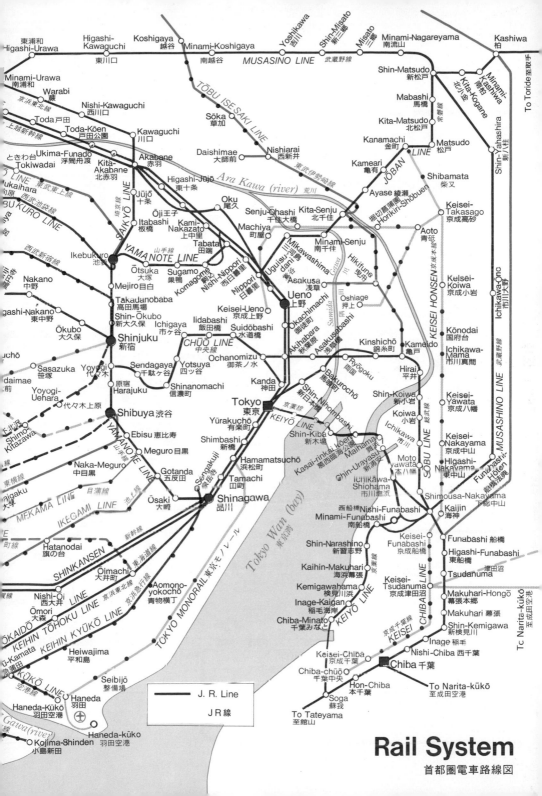

Rail System

首都圏電車路線図

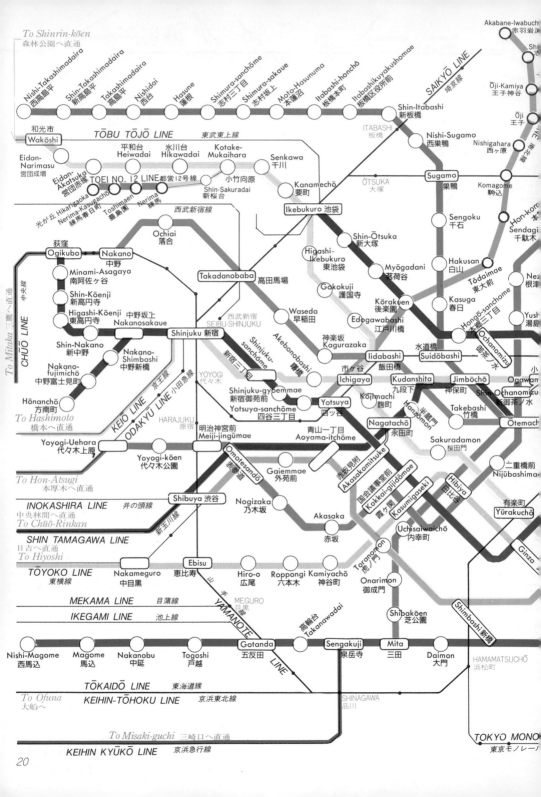

Subway System
東京地下鉄路線図

武動物公園へ直通
Tobu-Dōbutsukōen

TŌBU ISESAKI LINE
東武伊勢崎線

北千住
Kita-Senju

Kita-Ayase
北綾瀬

Ayase
綾瀬

To Toride 取手へ直通

JŌBAN LINE 常磐線

To Inzai-Makinohara
印西牧の原へ直通

町屋
Machiya

JŌBAN LINE 常磐線

KEISEI LINE 京成線

南千住
Minami-Senju

TŌBU ISESAKI LINE
東武伊勢崎線

TA

hi-Nippori
日暮里

NIPPORI
日暮里

Minowa
三ノ輪

Iriya
入谷

押上
Oshiage

To Narita Airport 成田空港へ直通

田原町
Tawaramachi

Honjo-
azumabashi
本所吾妻橋

Ueno 上野

Asakusu 浅草

Inaricho
稲荷町

KEY TO LINES (SEN)
凡例

ohirokoji
上野広小路

Nakaokachimachi
仲御徒町

Kuramae
蔵前

GINZA LINE
銀座線

UKACHIMACHI
御徒町

ehirochō
末広町

MARUNOUCHI LINE
丸ノ内線

Akihabara
秋葉原

Asakusabashi
浅草橋

HIBIYA LINE
日比谷線

iichō
路町

Iwamotochū
岩本町

KINSHICHŌ
錦糸町

Motoyawata
本八幡

MUSASHINO LINE
武蔵野線

西船橋
Nishi-Funabashi

TŌZAI LINE
東西線

Kanda 神田

Bakuro-
Yokoyama
馬喰横山

Higashi-
Nihombashi
東日本橋

SŌBU LINE 総武線

To Tsudanuma
津田沼へ直通

CHIYODA LINE
千代田線

Mitsukoshi-
mae
三越前

Shinozaki
篠崎

Baraki-
nakayama
原木中山

YŪRAKUCHŌ LINE
有楽町線

Nihombashi
日本橋

Kodenmachō
小伝馬町

人形町 Ningyocho

Mizue
瑞江

HANZŌMON LINE
半蔵門線

京

Nihombashi
日本橋

Hamuchō
浜町

Ichinoe
一之江

Gyōtoku
行徳

TOEI ASAKUSA LINE
都営浅草線

atchōme
一丁目

Kyōbashi
京橋

Morishita
森下

Funabori
船堀

TOEI MITA LINE
都営三田線

Takarachō
宝町

Kayabachō 茅場町

Kikukawa
菊川

Higashi-Ōjima
東大島

Minami-Gyōtoku
南行徳

都営三田線

Shintomichō
新富町

Hatchōbori
八丁堀

Suitengū-mae
水天宮前

Sumiyoshi
住吉

Ojima
大島

Urayasu
浦安

TOEI SHINJUKU LINE
都営新宿線

Higashi-Ginza

Tsukiji
築地

Tsukishima
月島

Monzen-
nakachō
門前仲町

Nishi-Ōjima
西大島

Kasai
葛西

都営新宿線

Toyosu
豊洲

Kiba
木場

J.R. LINE
JR線

Tatsumi
辰巳

Nishi-Kasai
西葛西

OTHER LINE
その他の線

HANEDA-KŪKŌ
羽田空港

Shinkiba
新木場

Tōyōchō
東陽町

Minami-Sunamachi
南砂町

KEIYŌ LINE
京葉線

Junction Station
乗換駅

21

Ginza and Yurakucho

Perhaps the very meaning of the name Ginza, "the silver guild," best sums up Tokyo's original elegant quarter. After the opening of Japan to the outside world in the later part of the 1800s, Ginza became the first Westernized district in Tokyo, and the premier center for sightseers and shoppers. The gathering place of the chic, Ginza soon developed into a mecca of Western culture and fashion.

Its proximity to the centers of business, finance and government have always made Ginza an after-hours haunt for expense-account-laden businessmen and politicians. Business negotiations are conducted in countless high-class hostess clubs, which are discreetly tucked away in the neon-bathed back streets of Ginza.

During recent years, Ginza's image as a middle-aged town has tended to leave the young uninterested. But although more contemporary districts have replaced Ginza at the forefront of Tokyo fashion, it is still the home of some of

A theater and department store complex in Yurakucho

the leading department stores—including a branch of **Mitsukoshi**, which in 1904 became Japan's first with its Nihonbashi store. On one fashionable side street are found the likes of Gucci and Louis Vuitton while one of Ginza's first genuine cafes, **Fugetsudo**, is still open for business nearby. The **Yoshinoya** shoe store (3562-3871), whose reputation for serving the Imperial Family speaks for itself, was established at the turn of the century. Originally this shop sold only men's and children's shoes, but now carries women's footwear, ballet shoes and outfits, and general clothing. Also in Ginza is the **Eikokuya** (3561-3290), which sells made-to-order men's suits of imported English cloth. The **Ginza Melsa** building (3567-2131) is filled with boutiques and specialty shops, where you can find quality imported brands of women's clothing and accessories. The swank **Printemps**, **Seibu**, and **Hankyu** department stores have added new life to the area with recently opened branches. Nearby, at the Sukiyabashi Crossing, is the **Sony Building**, which is a favorite meeting place.

An exciting finale at Takarazuka Theater

Made interesting by continually changing exhibits inside and out, the building
houses the Sony and Nissan showrooms,
along with various boutiques, on floors
that step upwards in a spiral. In the
basement is a branch of the famed Paris
restaurant **Maxim's**, the camera shop
Hero, which stocks just about every camera made in Japan, plus a variety of Sony
products (3573-2371). Many of Tokyo's
top art galleries are found nearby. Just a
short walk from here, down Harumi Dori
toward Mitsukoshi, is the **Jena Bookstore**
(3571-2980), which has a good selection
of foreign books and magazines on the
third floor. Just a little farther down
Harumi Dori, directly in front of Higashi
Ginza subway station is the **Kabuki
Theater**, with its early seventeenth cen-
tury-style "Japanese baroque" building
dating back to 1924. Here one may see
gorgeous costumes, dynamic set changes,
and gifted *onna-gata* female impersonat-
ators on stage. Since the Edo period,
kabuki remains the most popular traditional performing art in Japan. A few
short blocks behind the Kabuki Theater

The lights of Ginza at dusk

is the pink- and silver-tiled **Magazine
Gallery**, housing a gallery of 1300 magazines from fifty-six countries, open to the
public free of charge (3545-7227).

Ginza's neighbors, Yurakucho and
Hibiya, comprise the heart of the business
and entertainment district. In Yurakucho,
located just across the train tracks from
Ginza, is the **Tourist Information Center**,

Currency and Foreign Exchange

Japanese paper currency consists of
¥10,000, ¥5,000, and ¥1,000 bills. There
are six different denominations of coins:
¥500, ¥100, ¥50, ¥10, ¥5, ¥1. Since the
introduction of the controversial consumption tax in April 1989, which has
in many cases done away with the convenient round-numbered shopping of
the past, the troublesome ¥5 and alu-
minum ¥1 coins have become quite common. It is a good idea to keep some of
the copper ¥10 coins on hand for local
telephone calls, while the silver-colored

¥500, ¥100, and ¥50 coins are useful for
the wide variety of vending machines
found all over Tokyo, including the ticket machines at the train stations.

To change dollars into yen, or vice ver-
sa, go to any of the city banks. Among
them, the Bank of Tokyo specializes in
foreign exchange service.

Though major credit cards are generally accepted at hotels, many restaurants,
and retail stores, a large number of other
establishments in Tokyo still only take
cash. If you're not sure, it's a good idea
to ask beforehand. There are no personal checks in Japan.

Hibiya Park is a paradise for strollers

American prescriptions. For a down-to-earth taste of Tokyo, you'll find outdoor *yakitori* (skewered chicken) booths under the tracks of the station, popular drinking spots frequented by office workers during the evening.

In nearby Hibiya the **Imperial Hotel**, one of Japan's oldest and finest, was founded in 1890. The predecessor of the current building was designed by Frank

The busy heart of Tokyo's Ginza

offering free maps and other information in English. Underneath Yurakucho Station is the **International Arcade**, where tourists can find Japanese products and other items at reasonable prices. The **American Pharmacy**, first opened in 1950, is also nearby. Offering household remedies and other products hard to find elsewhere in Japan, the store has an English-speaking staff, and will even fill

Essential Information

Time zone.
Japan is fourteen hours ahead of New York (Eastern Standard Time), and nine hour ahead of Greenwich Mean Time. Subtract one hour from the time difference during daylight savings time in the United States.

Climate and clothes.
Spring and fall in Tokyo offer the best weather, with comfortable temperatures and relatively low humidity. Summers are hot and humid. Winters produce little snow, and there is none of the bitter coldness frequently common in the North-

east cities of the U.S. June marks the beginning of the rainy season, which often lasts until the middle of July. Lightweight, breathable fabrics are essential during the summer. Business suits and ties are worn year round by Tokyo's office workers, even in the hot summer months, so it is best to dress conservatively. Casual dress is acceptable, however, since few Tokyo restaurants have dress codes.

Electric current.
Tokyo is 100–110 V, 50 cycles AC. Western Japan, including Kyoto, Osaka, and Nagoya, is 60 cycles AC.

Lloyd Wright, and now stands in Meiji Mura, an authentic museum village outside of Nagoya. Near the Imperial Hotel are big-name travel agencies and airlines. This area is known for the several prominent theaters, including the **Tokyo Takarazuka Gekijo**, famous for its all-female cast in Broadway-style musicals. **Hibiya Park**, next-door to the **Imperial Palace** (formerly Edo Castle, the stronghold of the Tokugawa Shogun), became Japan's first Western-style park in 1903. Originally the site of a feudal mansion, a section of the Edo Castle wall which ran along the moat still remains. Hibiya Park's cultural facilities include a classical music recital hall, two libraries, and an outdoor concert stadium.

The Kabukiza: a glimpse of traditional Japan in the Ginza

Public Phones and Postal Services

There are several types of public phones in Japan, each with a different color—green, yellow, red, aqua and pink. Local calls (within Tokyo) cost ¥10 for one minute in the daytime, and for 80 seconds between 11 P.M. and 8 A.M. You can put in several ¥10 coins in advance; unused coins will be returned. Long-distance calls within Japan can be made from any color phone, but green, yellow or red phones, which accept ¥100 coins, make long-distance calls much easier. All green phones also take telephone cards. These pre-paid plastic cards, about the size of a credit card but much thinner, can be purchased at vending machines often found near green telephones, and at small supermarkets and other shops throughout Japan. Direct overseas calls can be made from gray public phones or green ones that display a small globe symbol in gold.

Post offices are located throughout the city. Local post offices handle mail from 9:00 A.M. to 5:00 P.M., weekdays only, but main post offices, which are usually near major train stations, stay open longer (9:00 A.M. to 7:00 P.M. on weekdays), and are also open 9:00 A.M. to 3:00 P.M. on Saturdays and 9:00 A.M. to 12:30 P.M. on Sundays and national holidays. (The closing hours might differ slightly depending on the particular post office.) Take any urgent international mail to the International Post Office, a short walk from the Marunochi exit of Tokyo Station. It is open from 9:00 A.M. to 7:00 P.M. on weekdays, 9:00 A.M. to 5:00 P.M. on Saturdays, and 9:00 A.M. to 12:30 P.M. on Sundays and national holidays. Even outside these hours, if you want to send something by special delivery, there is a buzzer to call a clerk who will accept your mail. A letter weighing up to 20 g costs ¥110 to the U.S.

This is a map of the Nagatachō, Kasumigaseki area.

Grid labels (top): A B C D E
Grid labels (left): 1 2 3 4 5 6 7

SHINJUKU DŌRI (AVE.) 新宿通り

(5) (4) Kōjimachi 麹町 (3) (2) (1)

20 Employment Promotion Project Corp. 雇用促進事業団
Wacoal Kōjimachi Bldg ワコール麹町ビル
FM Tok エフエム東

Sophia (Jōchi) Univ. 上智大学
Kōsai Kaikan 弘済会館
Kōjimachi Dai Bldg 麹町ダイビル
Shuwa TBR Bldg 秀和TBRビル

Hanzōmon P.Sta.
Kōjimachi P.Sta.

(1)
Hanzōmon Line
半蔵門

Fukudaya, Japanese Restaurant 福田家
Kioichō Bldg 紀尾井町ビル
Park Bldg パークビル
Japan Foundation 国際交流基金
Bungeishunju 文芸春秋

Hirakawa Tenjin 平河天神
Hirakawachō 平河町

Hayabusac 隼町

Nat'l Thea 国立劇

Kioichō 紀尾井町
Shimizudani Park 清水谷公園
Hotel New Ōtani ホテルニューオータニ

Kōjimachi Kaikan 麹町会館
Nihon Toshi Center 日本都市センター
Nihon Toshi Center Hall 日本都市センターホール
Zenkyōren Bldg 全共連ビル
Kōjimachi Jr.H.Sch. 麹町中

(2)
Hōchi Newspaper 報知新聞
Japan Junior Chamber 日本青年会議所

Engei Hall 演芸場
Supr 最

Benkei-bori (moat) 弁慶濠
SHUTO EXPWY NO.4

Hotel New Ōtani Tower ホテルニューオータニタワー
Tower 新館
Benkei-bashi 弁慶橋

Guest House 旧館
Akasaka Prince Hotel 赤坂プリンスホテル

Sabō-kaikan Hall 砂防会館ホール
Sabō Kaikan 砂防会館
Metropolitan District Hall (To-do-fu-ken Kaikan) 都道府県会館

Towns & Villages Kaikan 全国町村会館
IBM
Liberal-Democratic Party H.Q. 自由民主党本部

SOTOBORI DŌRI (AVE.) 外堀通り
首都高速4号線

Akasaka-mituke NAGATACHO 永田町
赤坂見附
Official Residence of the Speaker of the House of Representatives 衆議院議長公邸

Official Residence of the President of the House of Councillors 参議院議長公邸

Nagatachō 永田町
Kōjimachi 永田町小
Nagatachō E.Sch. 永田町小

NAGATACHŌ 永田町

Maeda Surgery Hosp 前田外科医院
Suntory Bldg サントリービル
Suntory Mus. of Art サントリー美術館

Moto-Akasaka 元赤坂
(1)

Kajima Bldg 鹿島ビル
AIU Akasaka Bldg AIU赤坂ビル
Belle Vie Akasaka ベルビー赤坂

Akasaka Tōkyū Hotel 赤坂東急ホテル

Embs. of Argentina, Lebanon, Jordan アルゼンチン、レバノン、ヨルダン大使館

(2)
Akasaka Public Hall 赤坂公会堂
Toyokawa Inari 豊川稲荷

Fuji Bank 富士
Akasaka-fudōson 赤坂不動尊

Sannō Grand Bldg 山王グランドビル
Emb. of Mexico メキシコ大使館

Members' Office House of Councillors 参議院議員会館

AOYAMA DŌRI (AVE.) 青山通り 246
Toraya 虎屋
Akasaka Police Sta. 赤坂署
Akasaka Public Hall 赤坂公会堂

(3)
HITOTSUGI DŌRI 一ツ木通り
AKASAKA-MITSUKE 赤坂見附

Hibiya H. Sch. 日比谷高校

Nagatachō 永田町

Bldg two Members' Office House of Representat 衆議院第二議員会館

(4)
Yamawaki Gakuen (Sch.) 山脇学園
Jōdo-ji 浄土寺
Jōgen-ji 常玄寺

Sumitomo Seimei Akasaka Bldg 住友生命赤坂ビル
Kokusai Sannō Bldg 国際山王ビル

Hie Jinja (shrine) 日枝神社
Capitol Tōkyū Hotel キャピトル東急ホテル
Sannō Hanten 山王飯店

Bldg one Members' Office House of Representatives 衆議院第一議員会館

MINATO-KU 港区
Nippon Colombia 日本コロムビア
Akasaka 赤坂

Sanyō Akasaka Bldg サンヨー赤坂ビル
Sannōshita 山王下
Sakura Bank さくら銀行

Hoshigaoka Bldg 星が岡ビル
Petroleum Communication Center 石油資料館

KOKKAI-GIJIDO 国会議事
Science Bldg サイエンスビル
Prime Minis Official Resid 首相官邸

Entsū-ji 円通寺
TBS 東京放送
TBS Hall TBSホール

Yachiyo Bldg 八千代ビル
Sumitomo Bank 住友銀行

Kokusai Akasaka Bldg 国際赤坂ビル
Nisshō Iwai 日商岩井

Tokyo Isuzu Motor 東京いすゞ

Akasaka Shanpia Hotel 赤坂シャンピアホテル
TBS Golf Studio TBSゴルフスタジオ
Minato Shinkin Bank (H.O.) 港信金(本店)
Kokusai Shin Akasaka Bldgs 国際新赤坂ビル
East Bldg 東館
West Bldg 西館

GINZA LINE 銀座線
Toshiba EM 東芝EM
French Trans
Komatsu Bldg 小松ビル
Tame

Nagatachō, Kasumigaseki
永田町　　　霞が関

1:8,000
0　　　　　　300m

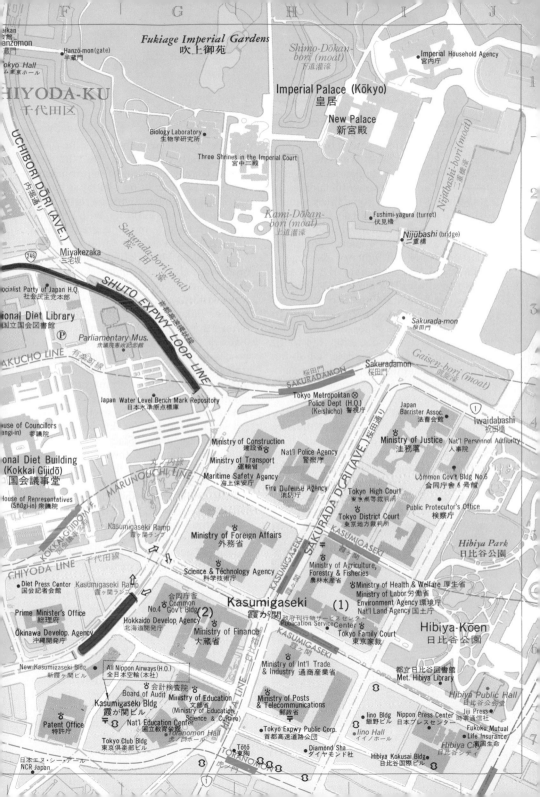

Kasumigaseki and Nagatacho

On the south side of the Imperial Palace, just west of Hibiya Park, is Kasumigaseki, the center of Japanese officialdom. In this district there are some thirty administrative and judicial offices of the Japanese government, including the powerful Ministries of Justice, Finance, and International Trade and Industry. During the Edo period, this stronghold of Edo Castle was the site of the mansions of those Tokugawa hereditary retainers who were feudal lords in their own right, and to whom all important government functions were reserved. After the Meiji Restoration this area was reserved for the military. Kasumigaseki did not become the home of Japanese governmental offices until after the Great Earthquake of 1923.

While most of Kasumigaseki today consists of modern highrises, the **Ministry of Justice Building**, completed in 1895, was designed by two Berliners at the height of Western-style construction in Japan. The original roof, unfortunately, was destroyed by fire during World War II.

The **Kasumigaseki Building**, Japan's first skyscraper, was completed in 1968. It stands only thirty-six stories (482 feet) high, because earthquake requirements prevented construction of a taller building. Besides offices, there are restaurants and shops in the building, with the thirty-sixth floor offering a panoramic view of the Imperial Palace.

The **Tokyo Metropolitan Police Headquarters** is also in Kasumigaseki. It is the eighteen-story building directly facing **Sakuradamon Gate** of the Imperial Palace. Sakuradamon is the famous spot where the Shogun's powerful Regent Ii Naosuke was assassinated as his armed procession was leaving the castle grounds one unusually snowy morning in the spring of 1860. Historians credit the event with hastening the downfall of the Tokugawa Shogunate. To see this historical spot, take the Yurakucho Subway Line to Sakuradamon Station.

The high ground southwest of the Imperial Palace is Nagatacho, the center of Japanese national politics. Here, surrounding the **Diet Building**, are the Prime Minister's Official Residence, the Prime Minister's Office, the Members' Office Buildings of the House of Representatives and the House of Councilors, and the headquarters of the various political parties.

The Japanese Diet, the sole lawmaking organ of the country, consists of two chambers: the lower House of Representatives, and the upper House of Councilors. The more powerful Lower House has 511 seats, to which members are elected to four-year terms. The Upper House holds 252 seats, to which members are elected to six-year terms. The Diet building, completed in 1936, was modelled after European and American statehouses. To get there, take either the

The Diet Building, with its distinct architecture

Marunouchi or the Chiyoda Line to Kokkaigijido-mae Station (Kokkaigijido means "Diet Building"; the suffix *mae*, [in] "front" [of]). For admittance, show your passport at the reception desk. (Open 8:00 A.M.–5:00 P.M.; closed second and fourth Saturdays, Sundays, and holidays.)

Just north of the Diet Building is the **Diet Library**. Here, in the nation's largest library, are a total of 3,575,053 Japanese-language books and 1,478,699 books in foreign languages (figures as of December 31, 1989) available for reference. (3581-2331; Open 9:30 A.M.–5:00 P.M.; closed second and fourth Saturdays, Sundays and holidays.)

Also in Nagatacho is the **Water Level Branch Mark Repository**, another Meiji-era treasure. Calculating from a point 80.3 feet above the average water level of the Sumida River, this serves as the standard by which all geographical elevations in Japan are measured.

The **National Theater of Japan** (3265-7411) is a seven- or eight-minute walk from Nagatacho Station. (Take the number four exit from the station.) Built to promote traditional dramatic arts, the basic design of this theater, which was

The Imperial Palace

modeled after a log house in the Todaiji Temple complex in Nara, dates back several centuries. Its large auditorium features kabuki, and the small auditorium *bunraku* (puppet plays). Engei Hall is an intimate theater for *rakugo* (comic storytelling), *manzai* (comic stage dialogue) and recitals. Inquire at the theater ticket office, any Pia Station, or see "Useful Telephone Numbers" (Ticket Saison) for program information and ticket availablility.

Asking Directions		
	bookstore	*honya*
	coffee shop	*kissaten*
Where's JR station?	pharmacy	*yakkyoku*
JR eki wa doko desuka?	police box	*koban*
Where's the subway station?	post office	*yubinkyoku*
Chikatetsu eki wa doko desuka?	restaurant	*resutoran*
Where's the ANA Hotel?	taxi	*takushi*
ANA hoteru wa doko desuka?	train	*densha*
Where's the restroom?	straight	*massugu*
O-te-arai wa doko desuka?	left	*hidari*
Where's the telephone?	right	*migi*
Denwa wa doko desuka?	here	*koko*
	there	*soko*
	over there	*asoko*

Marunouchi, Ōtemachi
丸の内 大手町

1:6,000

300m

Uchi Kanda 内神田 (3)

Uchi Kanda 内神田 (2)

Uchi Kanda 内神田 (1) 一丁目

Kanda Nishikichō 神田錦町 (1)

Kanda Nishikichō 神田錦町 (2)

(3)

SOTOBORI DŌRI (AVE.)

MARUNOUCHI LINE

SHUTO EXPWY 'LOOP LINE

Kikkōman キッコーマン

Hitachi Bldg 日立ビル

Kandabashi Ramp 神田橋ランプ

Coop Bldg コープビル

Chiyoda Ward Office 千代田区総合庁舎

Time-Life Bldg タイム・ライフビル

Otemachi NTT Bldg 大手町NTTビル

Norin Chukin Bank 農林中金

Nihon Keizai Newspapers 日本経済新聞

Nikkei Hall 日経ホール

JA Bldg JAビル Nōkyō Hall 農協ホール

Sankei Newspapers 産経新聞

Sankei Kaikan (hall) サンケイ会館

Federation of Economic Orgs 経団連

Japan Development Bank 日本開発銀行 KDD Otemachi Bldg KDD大手町ビル

Kōko Bldg 公庫ビル

New Kōko Bldg 新公庫ビル

Yomiuri Newspapers 読売新聞

Tokyo Immigration Bureau 東京入国管理局 Gov't Publication Service Center 大手町政府刊行物サービスセンター

NO.1 NO.2 NO.3

Common Gov't Bldgs 合同庁舎

Meteorological Agency 気象庁

Tokyo Fire Dept 東京消防庁 Marunouchi Fire Sta. 丸の内消防署

Hill of Masakado's Head (Masakado Kubizuka) 将門首塚

Mitsui Mutual 三井生命ビル

Mitsui Bussan Bldg 三井物産ビル

Maruha マルハ本社

Long-Term-Credit Bank of Japan 日本長期信用銀行

Ōte Center Bldg 大手センタービル

IBM Info. Sci. Musm IBM情報科学館

Asahi Bank(H.O.) あさひ銀行(本店)

Sanwa Bank 三和銀行

NKK Bldg NKKビル

AIU Bldg AIUビル

Export-Import Bank of Japan 日本輸出入銀行 K.K.B Tokyo Takebashi K.K.B東京竹橋

Marubeni (H.O.) 丸紅本社

Mainichi Newspapers 毎日新聞

Bronze Statue of Kusunoki Masashige 楠木正成像

TAKEBASHI 竹橋

Hosp. of Imperial Household Agency 宮内庁病院

Imperial Guard Sch. 皇宮警察学校

Cabinet Library (Naikaku Bunko) 内閣文庫

Imperial Guard H.Q. 皇宮警察本部

Site of Edo Castle 江戸城跡

East Imperial Garden (Kōkyo Higashi Gyoen) 皇居東御苑

Chiyoda 千代田

Ote-mon 大手門

Ote-bori (moat) 大手濠

Kikyo-bori (moat) 桔梗濠

Nihombashi-Hongokuchō 日本橋本石町

EDO DŌRI (AVE.) 江戸通り

Tokiwa E. Sch. 常盤小

Shin-Tokiwa-bashi (Br.) 新常盤橋

Bank of Japan (Nippon Ginko) 日本銀行 (本店)

Tokiwabashi Park 常盤橋公園

Tokiwa-bashi (Br.) 常盤橋

Nippon Steel Bldg 新日鉄ビル

Daiwa Securities 大和証券

Asahi Tokai Bldg 朝日東海ビル

Nippon Bldg 日本ビル

Tokai Bank 東海銀行

Ōtemachi 大手町 (2) 二丁目

Ōtemachi 大手町 (1) 一丁目

OTEMACHI

HANZOMON LINE 半蔵門線

SOBU LINE 総武線

SOTOBU LINE 総武線

UCHIBO LINE

TOZAI LINE 東西線

Tokyo International P.O. 東京国際郵便局

Postal Services Bureau 東京郵政局 Postal Inspection Bureau 関東郵政監察局

Communications Musm 逓信総合博物館

NTT Date Otemachi Bldg NTTデータ大手町ビル New Otemachi Bldg 新大手町ビル

Urbannet New Otemachi Bldg アーバンネット新大手町ビル

NTT Marunouchi NTT丸の内

New Ōtemachi Bldg 新大手町ビル

Nomura Bldg 野村ビル

Daiwa bldg 大和ビル

Fuji Bank 富士銀行 (本店)

Tōyō Trust 東洋信託銀行 (本店)

Citibank シティバンク

Ōtemachi Bldg 大手町ビル

Ōtemachi First Square 大手町ファーストスクエア

CDP Bldg CDPビル

Sumitomo Bank 住友銀行

Tokyo H.O. 東京銀行 Bank of Tokyo 東京銀行 (本店)

Sumitomo Trust 住友信託銀行

Bank Hall 銀行会館

Industrial Bank of Japan 日本興業銀行 (本店)

Marunouchi Hotel 丸の内ホテル

JTB

Marunouchi Center Bldg 丸の内センタービル

EITAI DŌRI (AVE.) 永代通り

Palace Hotel パレスホテル

Marunouchi and Otemachi

*J*ust north of Hibiya and Yurakucho is the Marunouchi district, which, combined with Otemachi to the north, encompasses the financial center of Tokyo. Meaning "within the moat" (of old Edo Castle's outer moat), Marunouchi is on the east side of the Imperial Palace, and was once the site of mansions of the Shogun's most elite retainers. Otemachi is built around an area which was formerly the Ohte Gate, just inside of which was located the government's financial office in the days of the Tokugawa Shogunate. While Otemachi was selected as the site for the new Home Ministry and Treasury Building with the advent of the Meiji Restoration (1868), neighboring Marunouchi was used as a military parade ground, until 1890, when the Mitsubishi Corp. purchased it at a low cost. After this, Marunouchi sat idle for decades, until the construction of **Tokyo**

Tokyo Station's classic exterior

Station in 1914, when the area experienced a building boom.

While modern Tokyo is largely a labyrinth of narrow one-way streets, winding back alleys, small passageways, and cubbies, the wide lanes and boulevards of the Marunouchi and Otemachi districts form well-ordered, right-angled blocks, giving a no-nonsense air to Tokyo's major business center. Here are located not only the headquarters of the

---

Vending Machines for Train Tickets

Commuter train tickets in Tokyo are sold through vending machines. All machines accept ¥10, ¥50 and ¥100 coins, and many take ¥500 coins and ¥1,000 bills as well. (If the machine does not take bills, there should be a change machine nearby for ¥1,000 bills.) Since fares vary depending on the distance traveled, it would be a good idea to know the fare to your destination in advance. (There is always a map of fare destinations posted near the vending machines, but the place names are generally written only in Japanese.) If you don't know the fare to your destination, purchase the cheapest ticket—the prices differ depending upon the railroad company or subway system—and pay the balance at the other end, either at the gate or at the fare adjustment window. To buy a ticket, simply deposit the proper amount of money (the amount you have deposited will appear on the machine), and press the appropriate fare button. (These buttons are divided into two groups; the lower priced buttons are for children, the others for adults.) Your ticket and change will come out through the slot at the bottom of the machine. When passing through the ticket gate, let the attendant punch your ticket, which you will surrender upon exiting the station of your destination.

largest Japanese corporations and banks, but also branch offices of powerful foreign financial institutions. The section of Marunouchi in front of Tokyo Station has joined London's City and New York's Wall Street as a center of international financial activity.

In addition to the red-bricked Marunouchi Exit of Tokyo Station, which is on the eastern side of Otemachi, landmarks of these districts include the **Tokyo Station Hotel**. Moderately priced, this hotel opened the same year as the station itself; its high ceilings and tiled bathrooms add to its Meiji-era charm. One of the jewels of European-styled office buildings in Japan is the Marunouchi's **Meiji Seimei Building**; built in 1934, it was used by the U.S. Air Force after the war. The only other major financial institution in the area which uses a pre-World War II building as its

Going to work in Japan's financial center

headquarters is the **Dai-Ichi Mutual Life Insurance Company**. This building, facing the Imperial Palace Moat near Hibiya Park, served as headquarters for General Douglas MacArthur after the war. The **Mitsui Bussan Building** is famous for the wild spot-billed ducks which delight Tokyoites every spring in the small manmade pond in the front of the building.

Taxis

Tokyo's taxis are clean and safe, but while convenient (except during rush-hour traffic), the fare might easily add up to an amount that will give you pause. The daytime charge is ¥650 for the first two kilometers (1.24 miles), with incremental increases of ¥80 every 280 meters (308 yards). At night (11:00 P.M.–5:00 A.M) the initial fare is the same ¥650, but only for the first 1,538 meters (1,683 yards). The meter goes up ¥80 for every additional 215.4 meters (237 yards). There is an additional daytime charge when the taxi is moving less than 10 kph. This time charge in-creases by 30 percent at night.

If you are out until late at night (most train and subway lines stop running be-

tween midnight and 1:00 A.M.), the taxi may well be your only mode of transportation. One word of caution: hailing a cab after 11:00 P.M. in Tokyo's major night-life districts can become a major feat, particularly on weekends and holidays. If you should find yourself caught in such a predicament, step into the nearest pub or coffee shop, and relax until after 2:00 A.M. It will be easier to find an unoccupied taxi at that hour. Unoccupied cabs display two red lights above the dashboard on the passenger's side, which are easily visible from the street.

Since few taxi drivers speak English, it is best to have your destination written down in Japanese before you start. (There should be no problem if you are heading to your hotel or a well-known landmark.)

Shinjuku 新宿

Underground Arcade & Passage
地下街と地下道路

✿ Kojimaya Confectionery
小島屋乳業製菓

Kashiwagi Bldg
柏木ビル

Shinjuku
Health Cente
新宿保健

Naruko Tenjinsha
鳴子天神社

Jōon-ji
浄善寺

☆ Yodobashi
Daiichi E. Sch.
淀橋一小

Tokyo Language S
東京外語専門学

Shōko Chukin Bank
商工中金ビ

Nishi-Shinjuku (8)
西新宿8丁目

Yodobashi Daiichi Kindergarten
淀橋第一幼稚園

Nihon Men's Apparel A
日本メンズ・アパレル
アカデミー

ŌME KAIDŌ (AVE.)
青梅街道

Yamaguchi Bank
山口銀行

Nishi-Shinjuku (7)
西新宿7丁目

Kashiwagi Park
柏木公園

Tōhō
東邦銀

Nishi-shinjuku KB Bldg
西新宿KBビル

Tenriism Central Shr.
天理教中央教会

Hyōgo Bank
兵庫銀行

Tokyo Cookery Academy
東京調理師専門学校

Daikan Plaza
ダイカンプラ

MARUNOUCHI LINE
丸ノ内線

Rōsai Kaikan (hall)
労済会館

Yamagata Shiawase Bank
山形しあわせ銀行

Jōen-ji
常円寺 卍

Star Hotel Tokyo
スターホテル東京

Tokyo
東京

Tokyo Medical College Hospital
東京医科大学病院

Nishi-Shinjuku (6)
西新宿6丁目

Jōfū-ji
浄風寺

Shinjuku Island Tower
新宿アイランドタワー

Shinjuku Police Sta.
新宿署

Shinjuku Cookery Academy
新宿調理師専門学校

Shinjuku Nomura Bldg
新宿野村ビル (50Fl)

Free Observatory
無料展望ロビー (50Fl)

Nomura Hall
野村ホール(B1)

Yasuda Kasai-Kaijo Bldg (43Fl)
安田火災海上本社ビル

Togo Seiji Art Museum
東郷青児美術館(42Fl)

Tokyo Mode Academy
東京モード学園

Heiwa Credit Union
平和信組

Shōwa Shinkin
昭和信金

Odakyū
小田急ハ

Tokyo Hilton Int'l
東京ヒルトンインターナショナル

Shinjuku Kokusai Bldg
新宿国際ビル

Waterworks Musm
東京都水道記念館

Met. Bureau of Waterworks
都水道局(支)(Branch Office)

KITA DŌRI (AVE.) 北通り

Sakura Bank
さくら銀行

Shinjuku Mitsui Bldg
新宿三井ビル (55Fl)

Observation Restaurant
展望レストラン(54-55Fl)

Shinjuku Center Bldg
新宿センタービル (54Fl)

Free Observatory
無料展望台(53Fl)

Asahi Seimei Hall
朝日生命ホール

Sanwa Bank
三和銀行

Shinjuku L Tower
新宿Lタワー

Sumitomo Bank
住友銀行

Matsuoka Centra
松岡セントラ

Subaru Bldg
スバルビ

Green Tower Bldg
グリーンタワービル

Shinjuku Daiichi
Seimei Bldg
新宿第一生命ビル

Do Sports Plaza
ドゥスポーツプラザ

Shinjuku Sumitomo Bldg
新宿住友ビル (52Fl)

Free Observatory
無料展望台(51Fl)

Asahi Culture Center
朝日カルチャーセンター

Sumitomo Hall (B1)
住友ホール

Asahi Mutual Life
Insurance (H.O.)
朝日生命本社ビル

Dai-Ichi
Kangyō Bank
第一勧銀

西新宿1丁目

Nishi-Shinjuku(1)

Hotel Century Hyatt
ホテルセンチュリー
ハイアット

Hiroshima Bank
広島銀行

CHŪŌ DŌRI (AVE.)
中央通り

Shinjuku Bldg
新宿ビル

Meiji Seimei Bldg
明治生命ビル

Yasuda Seimei Bldg
安田生命ビル

Fuji Bank
富士銀行

West E

Yasuda Seimei Hall
安田生命ホール

Shinjuku P.O.
新宿局

Hokkaido Bank
北海道銀行

Highway Bus Terminal
高速バスターミナル

Yodobashi Camera
ヨドバシカメラ

Mitsubishi

Keio Plaza
Hotel (47Fl)
京王プラザホテル

Met. Assembly Hall
都議会議事堂

Keiō Plaza Hotel
(South Tower)
京王プラザホテル南館

Plaza Dōri
プラザ通り

Kadoya Hotel
かどやホテル

Yamanashi Chūō Bank
山梨中央銀行

東洋信託
Tōyō Trust

Industrial Bank of Japan
興銀

Sakuraya Camera
カメラのさくらや

Nishi-Shinjuku (2)
西新宿2丁目

No. 1

Metropolitan
Government Office
東京都庁

Shinjuku Monolith
新宿モノリス

NTT Yodobashi
NTT淀橋

San'ei Bldg
サンエービル

Meihō Bldg
明宝ビル

People's Finance Corp.
国民金融公庫

Doi Camera
カメラのドイ

Shinjuku Sky Bldg
新宿スカイビル

Shinjuku
Central Park
新宿中央公園

No. 2

Shinjuku
NS Bldg (30Fl)
新宿NSビル

KDD Bldg (32Fl)
KDDビル

KDD P.O.
KDD内局

Taihei Bldg
大平ビル

Fukutoku Bank
福徳銀行

Sakura Bank
さくら銀行

Kubo Bldg
久保ビ

Tokyo Kaijo Bldg
東京海上ビル

Sakakibara Mem.
榊原記念病院

Tsunohazu-bashi
(Br.) 角筈橋

MINAMI DŌRI (AVE.)
南通り

Shinjuku Washington Hotel
新宿ワシントンホテル

KEIŌ SHIN-SEN (NEW LINE)
京王新線

KEIŌ LINE
京王線

Zenrōsai Kaikan
全労済会館

Hotel Sunr
ホテルサン

Shinjuku Park Tower
新宿パークタワー

Yoyogi
代々木

Shinjuku

onsidering the meaning of its name, "new lodgings," perhaps it seems strange that Shinjuku is known as the town that never sleeps. Things become clear, however, once you know that in 1697 "new lodgings" were built along the Kōshu Kaidō road in the western outskirts of Edo, where today stands **Shinjuku Station**, the busiest in the world. In the eighteenth and nineteenth centuries this area was called "Naito Shinjuku," after the feudal lord Naito Kiyoshige. A station along the Koshu Kaido, Naito Shinjuku began prospering in the 1700s. General stores, tea-houses, and inns satisfied the needs of the many travelers to this first station along the main road connecting Edo to the provinces of Musashi and Kai. Today, some two million people pass daily through this station, into which converge eight train and subway lines, including the Yamanote, Chuo, Odakyu, Keio, and Marunouchi. The west end of Shinjuku Station is a terminal for thirty

Shinjuku boasts some of the tallest office buildings in the city

bus routes, just a five-minute walk from the highly visible skyscrapers of West Shinjuku. The first of these futuristic towers of modern architecture, the **Keio Plaza Hotel**, was completed in 1971. Its **Pole Star Bar**, 525 feet above ground, offers a great view of the city. The new **Tokyo Metropolitan Government Office** surpasses Ikebukuro's Sunshine 60 building as the nation's tallest structure.

While West Shinjuku is all skyscrapers, wide avenues, and just a touch of congestion, the east side of Shinjuku Station is what makes this area the pleasure capital within Tokyo. A bustling business and shopping district by day, East Shinjuku metamorphosizes into a gaudy, neon-soaked, and, for many, exciting experience by night. Around its maze of backstreets covering a relatively wide area, are thousands of bars, pubs, nightclubs, and restaurants. Even the video game centers, bowling alleys, cinemas and coffee shops here stay open late. In one almost hidden pocket, surrounded on three sides by the Hanazono Shrine, an elementary school, and an electric power company substation, is a quiet little row of back streets called **Goruden Gai**, or "Golden Street." Lined with tiny bars, most of which can't seat more than ten people, Goruden Gai was built in 1948 before prostitution was outlawed. Today it is the hangout of artists and writers, and still retains much of the seedy atmosphere of old.

At the very heart of Shinjuku's nightlife district is **Kabuki-cho**, Japan's most noted pleasure district. Here, in this concrete and neon garden of sensual delights the night is always bright. There are also many restaurants, night clubs, pubs, cinemas, and theaters. Kabuki-cho

Shinjuku Gyoen, noted for its stately groves

was named after the traditional Japanese dramatic form (it means "Kabuki-town") because it was slated to become the new site of the burned out Kabuki Theater in Ginza after the war. The plan was never realized, but the name stuck just the same.

Shinjuku is also a noted place for shopping. Adjacent to the station on the west side are the **Odakyu** and **Keio** department stores. On the south side of the station is **Lumine**, a conglomerate of boutiques and restaurants. **My City**, also filled with boutiques and small shops, is on the station's east side. Just outside the east exit, along Shinjuku Dori, is **Takano**, a fashion boutique building with a high-quality fruit store and delicatessen on the upper-basement level. On the sixth floor are restaurants serving foods from six different countries. Just up the street from Takano are three more big-name department stores: **Mitsukoshi**, **Marui** (which is separated into a number of buildings), and **Isetan**. The latter has a counter for foreign customers which gives shopping information in several languages. Extending underground on the east side of the station is the *Sabunado*, or in plain English "subterranean promenade." This long shopping corridor is filled with hundreds of stores, including a wide range of boutiques, restaurants, and coffee shops. There are also several camera shops in the area which offer some of the best prices in Tokyo. On the west side are **Yodobashi Camera**, **Doi Camera**, and **Sakuraya**; on the east side Sakuraya's main store, and a branch of Yodobashi.

A popular meeting spot is **Studio Alta**, with a giant video sign atop, which you can't miss when coming from the east exit of Shinjuku Station. On the fifth floor of this building is another **Pia Station**, an outlet for purchasing movie, theater, and concert tickets. Just down Shinjuku Dori is an equally popular rendezvous spot—the square at the foot of the escalator leading up to **Kinokuniya Bookstore**. On the fifth floor of this usually crowded bookstore is a wide selection of English-language books.

Shinjuku Gyoen garden, formerly the location of Lord Naito's eighteenth-century estate, is four times the size of Hibiya Park. An idyllic garden where the Tokyoite can escape from the hustle and bustle of the city, it houses 1,900 trees, including sixty-five varieties of cherries. The French and Japanese gardens, and the greenhouses with 670 varieties of orchids are definitely worth seeing. Before the war Shinjuku Gyoen was one of Japan's Imperial Palace Gardens, but was converted into a public park in 1948. In 1989 the funeral of the Emperor Showa was held here. Take the Marunouchi Subway Line to Shinjuku Gyoen-mae Station, or alternatively, walk for about fifteen minutes from the south exit of Shinjuku Station. (Open 9:00 A.M.–4:30 P.M.; closed Mondays; admission: ¥160.)

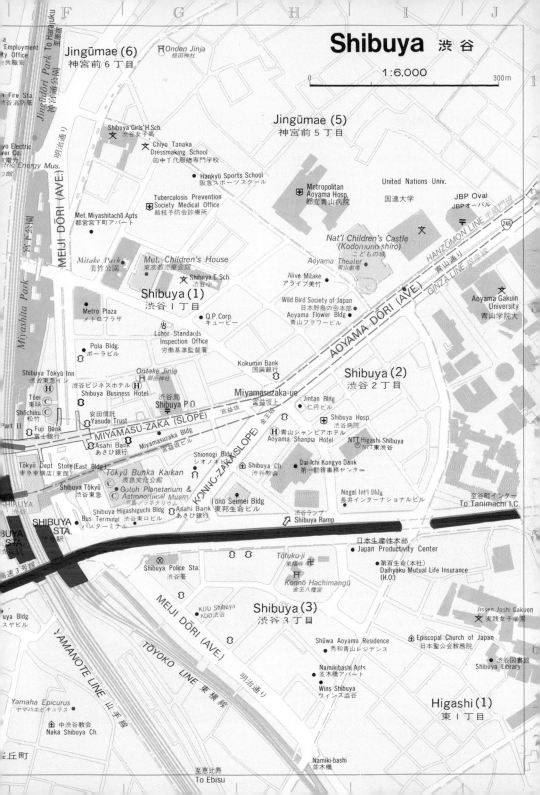

Shibuya

I n a city which seems to be undergoing a constant state of change, it is heartening to know that there is at least one thing that remains the same. **Hachiko Square** at the west end of Shibuya Station is always packed with people. This trend-setting area, where avant-garde Tokyo begins, is a convergence of energy overflowing with youth—a congregation of boutiques, department stores, restaurants, and theaters, and a super-terminal through which hundreds of thousands pass every day. Shibuya's symbol, the loyal Akita dog Hachiko—who from 1925 waited every day for ten years in front of the station for his dead master's return—is still commemorated with a bronze statue of the dog at the center of Hachiko Square, one of Tokyo's most noted meeting places.

At Shibuya Station, Japan's third busiest after Shinjuku and Ikebukuro, converge the Yamanote, Shin-Tamagawa, Inokashira, Toyoko, Ginza, and Hanzomon Lines. The station also serves as the terminal for over thirty bus routes.

Inside the station is **Tokyu** department store, whose main branch is just a five-minute walk away. Both of these stores have excellent gourmet sections, in the basement of the former, on the eighth floor of the latter. Directly across the street from the south exit is the eight-storied **Tokyu Plaza**, which in addition to boutiques, coffee shops, and a ninth floor filled with restaurants, has a branch of the **Kinokuniya Bookstore** (fifth floor) with a good selection of English-language books and magazines. (There is a larger English-language book selection at **Taiseido Bookstore** just down the street from Hachiko, next to MacDonald's.) Also

belonging to the Tokyu Group are four **109** department stores, all conveniently located near Shibuya Station. Among them is **Fashion Community 109**, a popular rendezvous spot for the young. An eight-storied conglomerate of ninety-two boutiques and restaurants, the exterior of the building is all postmodern glass and metal. On the second floor is a branch of **Pia Station** (Pia is the name of Tokyo's biggest event and entertainment magazine), a computerized ticket outlet for movies, concerts, plays, and sporting events. At the top is **109 Studio**, featuring live entertainment and giant video screens which pound out the latest international hits. **Parco**, up the street from Taiseido, is a complex of fashion boutiques, record stores, and restaurants frequented especially by young women. **Marui,** whose unique credit card installment plan has made it extremely popular among the young of both sexes, has two department stores nearby. Also in the immediate neighborhood are four **Seibu** department stores: the A and B Wings, which are connected to each other, the **Loft,** and the **Seed.** The eight-storied **Tokyu Hands** is the store for the do-it-yourself home-improvement, craft, and

Shibuya is a magnet for young people in Tokyo

hobby enthusiast. Having originally specialized in tools and materials, Tokyu Hands has since branched out into interior decoration and gifts. There is also a **Tower Records** nearby, the first Japanese branch of the famous Los Angles record store, which offers the largest stock of imports in the country.

Shibuya is not all shopping. Directly across the street from the north side of the station is **Tokyu Bunka Kaikan**, with four cinemas featuring first-run Western films. Next-door to the head branch of Tokyu department store is **Bunkamura**. Literally meaning "Culture Village," the building contains two cinemas, an art museum gallery, recording studios, a book store, and **Orchard Hall**, which is touted for its high-quality acoustics.

Shibuya has many eating options. In general, prices are reasonable and the food is eclectic. One interesting place to eat in is the imposing black **Prime Building**, which is right next to Fashion Community 109. Scattered among the many floors of the Prime Building are all sorts of restaurants and fast-food eateries, several of them offering ethnic cuisines, including Vietnamese, German, Korean and Southern European.

Just one stop away to the south from Shibuya on the JR Yamanote train line is Ebisu Station, which is connected by a moving walkway to **Yebisu Garden Place**. This is a pleasant and peaceful oasis for shopping, dining, and generally enjoying yourself. Yebisu Garden Place was built in 1994, and it is home to a Mitsukoshi department store, bakeries, cafés, cinemas, galleries, beer halls and restaurants with panoramic views, the Tokyo Westin Hotel, as well as the new restaurant and wine cellar of Joël Robuchon (the famous French chef), called **Taillevent Robuchon**.

The **NHK Broadcasting Center** is in

Yoyogi's National Gymnasium, the site of major events

Shibuya. In addition to the towering glass office building are the TV and radio buildings, one of which houses a museum. State-of-the-art technology—in twenty-two television studios, twenty-three radio studios, and eight dubbing studios—is used to broadcast NHK's five domestic stations throughout Japan, as well as to eighteen areas around the globe in twenty-one different languages. The multi-purpose **NHK Hall**, used for a wide variety of events such as the recording of television programs and concerts by the NHK Symphony Orchestra, is also part of the NHK Broadcasting Center. Guided tours lasting forty minutes are available. (Open daily, 10:00 A.M.–6:00 P.M.; closed second Monday every month.)

Also in Shibuya is the **National Gymnasium**. Located in **Yoyogi Park** (see Harajuku section), this structure is notable for its futuristic design by famous architect Kenzo Tange. Built for the swimming and basketball events of the 1964 Tokyo Olympics, the National Gymnasium includes an Olympic pool and an ice skating rink, both of which are open to the public in summer and winter, respectively.

F   G   H   I   J

ano Jinja

Aoyama Twin
(New Aoyama Bldg)
新青山ビル

Kōtoku-ji
高徳寺

Aoyama H. Sch.
青山高

Prince Chichibu Memorial
Rugby Stadium
秩父宮記念ラグビー場

CI Plaza
CIプラザ

Honda Motor(H.O.)
本田技研(本社)

Sumitomo Trust
住友信託

Nissan Fire &
Marine Insurance
日産火災海上

C. Itoh (Itochū) (Tokyo H.O.)
伊藤忠(東京本社)

Pola Aoyama Bldg
ポーラ青山ビル

Hotel President Aoyama
ホテルプレジデント青山

Kita-Aoyama(2)
北青山2丁目

mb. of Brazil
ジル大使館

Harajuku Ch.
原宿教会

Hazama Bldg
ハザマビル

AOYAMA DORI (AVE.) 青山通り

Asahi Bank
あさひ銀行

Aoba Park
青葉公園

Jihō-ji
持法寺

GAIENMAE 外苑前

NTT Aoyama
NTT青山

Akasaka Public
Health Center
赤坂保健所

Kaizō-ji Aoyama Sun-Crest
海蔵寺 青山サンクレスト

Aoyama Tower Bldg
青山タワービル

Gyokusōzen-ji
玉窓禅寺

Aoyama Bell Commons
青山ベルコモンズ

Baisō-in
梅窓院

Aoyama E. Sch.
青山小

Ryusen-ji
龍泉寺

Dai-Ichi Kangyō Bank
第一勧銀

Gaienmae P.O.
外苑前局

Aoyama Welfare Hall
青山福祉会館

Akasaka H. Sch.
赤坂高

Aoyama 3-chome
青山三丁目

Aoyama Metro Hall
青山メトロ会館

Akasaka Fire Sta.
赤坂消防署

Tōkyū Store
東急ストア

Plaza 246
プラザ246

a-kitamachi
chi (Apts)
北町団地

Japan Traditional Crafts Center
全国伝統的工芸品センター

Minami-Aoyama (2)
南青山2丁目

Bldg

Aoyama Peacock
青山ピーコック

Sumitomo Seimei Aoyama Bldg
住友生命青山ビル

Aoyama Mansion
青山マンション

Aoyama Cemetery
(Aoyama Reien)
青山霊園

Aoyama Ch.
青山教会

Kyōwa Bldg
協和ビル

Minami-Aoyama (3)
南青山3丁目

Seinan Welfare Hall
青南福祉会館

MINATO-KU
港区

Aoyama Funeral Hall
青山斎場所

Tokyo Aoyama Kaikan (hall)
東京青山会館

Science Council
of Japan
日本学術会議

Minami-Aoyama (4)
南青山4丁目

Aoyama Daiichi Mansion
第一マンション

Tessenkai Noh Theater
鉄仙会能楽研究所

Seinan E. Sch.
青南小

CHIYODA LINE 千代田線

Aoyama Social Education
Hall
青山社会教育会館

Aoyama Park
青山公園

u Moku Confectionnery
(H.O.)
ヨックモック(本社)

From 1st Bldg
フロムファーストビル

Akasaka Press Center
赤坂プレスセンター

nami-Aoyama(5)
南青山5丁目

La Collezione
コレッツィオーネビル

Nezu Art Musm
根津美術館

Nikka Whisky
ニッカウヰスキー

Kensetsu Kyōsai Kaikan
建設共済会館

GAIEN-NISHI DORI (AVE.) 外苑西通り

Nishi-Azabu(1)
西麻布1丁目

Kyōei Bldg
協栄ビル

Eihei-ji (temple), Tokyo
Branch (Chōkoku-ji)
永平寺東京別院(長谷寺)

Nishi-Azabu(2)
西麻布2丁目

Daian-ji
大安寺

Nishiazabu Welfare Hall
西麻布社会福祉会館

Daikannon
麻布大観音

Jigan-in
慈眼院

Nishi-Azabu P. O.
西麻布局

Nishi-Azabu
西麻布

Minami-Aoyama (6)
南青山6丁目

Emb. of Sudan
スーダン大使館

Fuji Photo Film (H.O.)
富士写真フィルム(本社)

Takagichō Ramp
高樹町ランプ

HUTO EXPWY No.3 首都高速3号線

Nishiazabu Bldg
西麻布ビル

Emb. of Ghana
ガーナ大使館

Harajuku, Aoyama
原宿   1:8,000   青山

mane Inn Aoyama
島根イン青山

0   300m

Harajuku and Aoyama

If Shibuya is where avant-garde Tokyo begins, its neighbor Harajuku—the mecca of Tokyo's young—brings it one step further, while the adjacent Aoyama epitomizes high-fashion in the Japanese capital. It is in this area that Tokyo's most exclusive boutiques are found and the leaders of Japanese fashion have their general headquarters.

Transversing Harajuku from Aoyama Dori is the zelkova-tree-lined **Omotesando**, one of the capital's most beautiful boulevards. This "Pilgrims' Way," as it translates, leads to **Meiji Shrine** (completed 1920), where the Emperor Meiji (1852–1912) is enshrined. Japan's largest wooden *torii* (shrine gate) stands magnificently at the entrance of the graveled walkway leading to the nation's most popular Shinto shrine, through which pour some four million people during a four-day period every New Year. Within its 17-acre (70,000-square-meter) precincts are some 170,000 trees, most of which are green all year round. The Inner Garden is known for its irises, which bloom in late spring, and its lily pond. The Treasure Museum exhibits photos and personal belongings of the Meiji Emperor and Empress (also enshrined here). (Open daily 5:40 A.M.–5:20 P.M. in spring and fall, 4:00 A.M.–5:00 P.M. in summer, 6:00 A.M.–4:00 P.M. winter; no admission charge to shrine.) Adjacent to Meiji Shrine is **Yoyogi Park**, which was the site of the Tokyo Olympic Village. Once inside its expansive 133-acre (540,000-square-meter) grounds, where the woods are a haven for birds, it is easy to forget that you are in Tokyo. On any Sunday afternoon the road running between the park and the **National Gymnasium** becomes a celebra-

Omotesando has been called Tokyo's Champs Elysées

tion of vintage American rock 'n' roll or some other music and dance performance currently capturing the imaginations of Japanese teenagers. *Takenoko-zoku*, or "Bamboo Shoot Kids," sporting black leather and greased black hair, started this tradition years ago, dancing defiantly in the open air to the hits of the Fifties.

Harajuku Station is one stop from Shibuya on the Yamanote Line. Constructed in 1924 in the style of the English countryside, the wooden station building reflects the flavor of the immediate area. The long, narrow street running from Harajuku Station, parallel to Omotesando, is **Takeshita Dori**, popular with the young throughout Tokyo. Lined with inexpensive clothing and accessory boutiques, fastfood restaurants, and coffee shops, this street gets extremely crowded on the weekends. On the corner of Meiji Dori and Omotesando is **Laforet**, a building overflowing with boutiques, which, like so much else in Harajuku, are geared to the adolescent crowd. The **Kiddyland** department store of toys is just past Meiji

Dori on Omotesando when coming from Harajuku Station. In addition to an extensive variety of toys, Kiddyland's six floors stock gifts and character goods, including the stars of Disney and Sesame Street. Just up the street is **Oriental Bazaar**, an antique store with a large stone Buddha at the entrance.

Further up Omotesando is Aoyama, which spreads out north and south with Aoyama Dori at its center. During the Edo period this area was the site of many temples, shrines, and samurai houses. After the Meiji Restoration it was used by the military. With the 1964 Olympics, high-rise buildings began lining Aoyama Dori, and today the district is home to a number of internationally famous fashion designers. Among them is Hanae Mori, who stocks her entire collection in the mirror-glass **Hanae Mori Building**, an Omotesando landmark. Issey Miyake, Japan's best known designer of both mens' and womens' clothes, has three different shops in this center of high fashion. **Kira Dori**, or Killer Street, so named by fashion designer Junko Koshino for its "killer shopping," is lined with trendy boutiques, cafes, and restaurants. Where Killer Street crosses Aoyama Dori is the popular fashion building **Aoyama Bell Commons**. In addition to its many boutiques, this popular meeting place has several restaurants and cafes, including a branch of **Sushisei**, a good chain for reasonably priced sushi.

On Aoyama Dori is **Kinokuniya International**, one of the few supermarkets in Tokyo which not only has an excellent selection of imported foods and wines, but where the signs are in English.

Backtracking to Harajuku, just off Omotesando, is the **Ota Museum of Art**, specializing in *ukiyoe* woodblock prints. The collection spans the complete history of *ukiyoe*, including such major artists as Kitagawa Utamaro, Toshusai Sharaku, Katsushika Hokusai, and Ando Hiroshige. (3403-0880; Open 10:30 A.M.–5:30 P.M.; closed Mondays, and each month from the 25th to the end; admission: ¥500.) The **Nezu Institute of Fine Arts** in Minami Aoyama specializes in old Japanese and Chinese works of art, including hanging scrolls, Buddhist scriptures, religious ornaments, sculpture, lacquer ware, tea ceremony utensils, textiles, and seven national treasures. (3400-2536; Open Tuesdays–Sundays 9:30 A.M.–4:30 P.M.; closed Mondays, holidays, in August, during New Year's holidays; admission: ¥1,000.) Among the area's numerous art galleries is Omotesando's **Spiral Garden**, an airy, open lobby which holds several exhibitions annually around the theme "Making Art Easier to Understand." (Open 11:00 A.M.–8:00 P.M. daily.)

Aoyama Cemetery is south of Aoyama Dori, near Killer Street. Japanese history buffs might enjoy walking around the precincts, as a good many historical figures are buried here. It is also a great place to view the cherry blossoms.

Meiji Shrine is noted for its elegant simplicity

Akasaka and Roppongi

*J*ust over the hill from the Diet is Akasaka, Tokyo's most sophisticated nightspot. Politicians and bureaucrats have traditionally patronized the black tile-roofed Japanese restaurants in Akasaka's exclusive geisha quarter, which is sometimes called the "back parlor" of Japanese politics. In fact, much of this district is indeed conservative—that is, before the sun goes down. This quiet neighborhood was the site of residences belonging to the Shogun's hereditary retainers during the Edo era. Along its narrow back streets are small shops, some generations old, selling kimono, lacquerware, china, and other traditional goods. Green grocers and other family-run stores add to the area's old-fashioned atmosphere, but after dark Akasaka transforms into a cosmopolitan garden of epicurean delights. Black limousines squeeze through narrow streets to exclusive restaurants. Businessmen on company expense accounts flock to Akasaka's chic supper clubs, cabarets, and expensive hostess clubs. Foreign VIPs and celebrities, both international and local, are wined and dined here. And travelers from all over the world fill some of the capital's finest hotels in Akasaka.

On the busy Akasaka-mitsuke crossing, through which runs the main avenue connecting Akasaka to Aoyama and Shibuya, is the **Akasaka Prince Hotel**. Hidden behind the hotel's glacial white newer annex is the elegant old wing, built in 1928 for a Korean prince. Across the street, behind the old moat, is the **Hotel New Otani**, whose fabulous gardens once belonged to the estate of the powerful Tokugawa Regent Ii Naosuke. The **Hotel Okura**, in nearby Toranomon, is another first-rate establishment with a large foreign clientele. This hotel stands on a promontory near the **United States Embassy**. Right in front is the **Okura Shūkokan Museum**, Japan's first private foundation museum. Here are works of art from all over Asia, such as swords, sculptures, paintings, traditional crafts, and Japanese *Noh* masks. Among the Japanese artifacts are many designated national treasures, important cultural properties, and important art objects. (3583-0781; Open 10:00 A.M.–4:00 P.M.; closed Mondays, unless a holiday; admission: ¥400.)

Across from Akasaka-mitsuke Station, through which run the Ginza and Marunouchi Subway Lines, is the **Suntory Museum of Art** (3470-1073). Located on the eleventh floor of the Suntory Building, its collection of over 2000 items includes many important artifacts from Japanese antiquity (genre paintings, clothing, furniture, tableware, etc.), and pieces designated national treasures and important cultural properties. (Open 10:00 A.M.–5:00 P.M.—Fridays to 7:00 P.M.; closed Mondays, unless a holiday; admission: ¥500.)

Roppongi: Tokyo's lively party town

For shopping, the **Belle Vie Akasaka** fashion boutique complex is located right over Akasaka-mistuke Station.

For a taste of something tradition-ally Japanese, **Toraya** (3408-4121) has been making *wagashi* (Japa-nese sweets) for hun-dreds of years. The house special, *kasho*, is said to have first been made as an offering to the Emper-or Ninmyo (810-850). Try one of the five kinds of fresh cakes made daily at the shop's tea room, where the menu changes with the season.

For an aesthetic appreciation of Japa-nese culture visit the

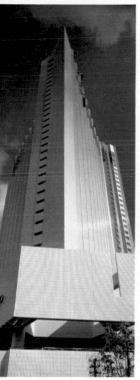

ANA Hotel Tokyo

Sogetsu Art Center (3408-1126), the mirrored-glass headquar-ters for the avant-garde Sogetsu school of flower arrangement on Aoyama Dori near the Canadian Embassy. The head of this school, Teshigawara Hiroshi, is per-haps best known as the director of the film *Woman of the Dunes*, based on Abe Kobo's novel of the same name. The **Sogetsu Art Museum** on the sixth floor contains the eclectic art collection of the school's late founder Teshigawara Sofu. Included are artifacts from China, Africa, Cyprus, India, and the Mayari civilization, and a seated statue of Bud-dha designated as an important cultural property. Among the modern and con-temporary artists represented are Leger, Picasso, Matisse, Braque, Okamoto Taro, and Kano Mitsuo. (3408-1126; Open weekdays and Saturdays 10:00 A.M.–5:00 P.M., closed Sundays, national and New Year's holidays, and between exhibits; admission: ¥500.)

South of Akasaka is the party town of Roppongi, where Tokyo nightlife begins and ends—early in the morning. Literally meaning "six trees," Roppongi is said to have been named after six resident feudal lords whose names included the Chinese character for "tree." Today, it is the noc-turnal playground of many a foreigner, as well as, of course, countless Japanese attracted by Roppongi's distinctively international atmosphere. The area has maintained its foreign image since 1945, when the American Occupation forces moved into the barracks which had been recently vacated by the Japanese Imperial Army. In fact, Roppongi has long been used by the military. The **Defense Agency** is headquartered here, near the blaring discos, night clubs, bars, restaurants, and boutiques which stay open all night long.

But for all its nightlife, one can't talk about Roppongi without mentioning **Ark Hills**, a kind of "futuristic mini-city." Here is the 900-room **Tokyo ANA Hotel**, its airy, greenery-filled atrium lobby com-plete with a waterfall. Also here are Asahi TV studios, 41 floors of office space, a luxury residential area and **Suntory Hall**—Tokyo's first hall designed and built exclusively for classical music concerts.

Japan's first music and film specialty store, **Wave Roppongi** (3408-0111), is also Tokyo's leading record shop. Known for its large quantity of imported CDs, Wave's specialist corners include Ethnic & World Music on the third floor, and a Mozart House on the fourth floor. It's located above Roppongi Station (Hibiya Line).

Hotels, Restaurants, Shopping and Nightlife

Tokyo ranks among the most cosmopolitan cities of the world, and its myriad hotels, department stores, boutiques, restaurants and the like are distinctly Japanese. In addition to covering traditional to international and ethnic establishments found in Tokyo, this section points out cultural differences the visitor is apt to encounter and places that cater to the needs of the foreign tourist and business person, and suggests carefully selected spots to suit a wide spectrum of tastes.

Tokyo Accommodations

*T*okyo is a city of hotels, almost 3,000 in fact. At the top of the list are the deluxe and first-class hotels, which, designed to serve foreign visitors and Japanese VIPs, include some of the world's best. They are typically large—some have as many as 2,000 rooms—have luxurious lobbies; first-class restaurants, bars, and boutiques; and an English-speaking staff. Travel agencies have offices in these hotels, and a pick-up service for guided tours is usually available. Business-service salons—offering translation, telexing, and faxing facilities, and other business-related assistance—are usually maintained. Prices generally start from around ¥29,000 (for a twin). The most expensive room in Tokyo is at the Imperial Hotel, where the 5,472-square-feet (509-square-meter) Imperial Suite costs ¥600,000 per night. The second costliest is at the New Otani, whose Deluxe Suite goes for ¥450,000 a night.

Standard hotels in Tokyo usually start from about ¥14,000 per person for a twin room. These hotels are generally smaller than the deluxe and first-class types with the number of rooms ranging anywhere from about 100 to 500. They don't have fancy lobbies, high-class restaurants, or business-service salons catering to foreigners. It is generally safe to say, however, that there will be some English-speaking staff at this class of hotel.

Next are so-called "business" hotels. These inexpensive establishments were developed to provide Japanese businessmen staying in town overnight with convenient, reasonable accommodations. Prices usually start from about ¥8,000 per night for a single. There is nothing fancy about them; in fact, they are downright spartan. They offer no spacious lobbies, and no room service. The rooms themselves are tiny, the bathrooms even tinier. But they are clean, and offer such conveniences as vending machines for toiletries, beer, whiskey, snacks, and so forth. The fare at the restaurant, which

ANA Hotel's seafood restaurant, Le Patio.

A Few Basic Japanese Phrases

Basic greetings

Good morning	*ohaiyo-gozaimasu*
Good afternoon	*konnichi-wa*
Good evening	*komban-wa*
Good night	*oyasumi-nasai*
Goodbye	*sayonara*

Other basic communication

Yes	*hai*
No	*i-eh*
Thank you	*arigato (gozaimasu)*
You're welcome	*do itashimashite*
Please	*onegaishimasu*
No, thank you	*kekko desu*
I'm sorry	*gomen-nasai*
Excuse me	*sumimasen*

Excuse me, do you speak English?
Sumimasen ga, eigo ga dekimasuka?
Excuse me, what is your name?
Sumimasen ga, onamae wa nan desuka?
My name is Smith.
Sumisu desu.

often doubles as a coffee shop during off-hours, and even triples as a bar at night, will be standard; and while the staff at a business hotel cannot be expected to speak English, you should have no language troubles checking in and out.

A unique experience in cheap accommodations, and an option used most frequently by Tokyo's male office workers to avoid the long commute home after a late night, are the so-called "capsule" hotels (about ¥4,000 per night). These consist of dozens of sleeping capsules built alongside and on top of each other. Each capsule is just large enough to fit one person—most comfortably lying down, has a color TV, alarm clock, air conditioner, sprinkler system and emergency button. Many capsule hotels are equipped with saunas, which are available for an extra charge.

While Western-style hotels are probably the best choice in the capital, a stay at a traditional Japanese inn (*ryokan*) is recommended at some point during a visit to Japan. Although Tokyo does have a few

The lobby at ANA Hotel

ryokan, the finer ones are found outside the city. A deluxe *ryokan* in the traditional style can cost as much, if not more than, a first-class hotel (¥15,000–¥35,000), but you will be provided with exquisite Japanese meals and bath (*o-furo*). The few *ryokan*-style establishments around Tokyo which are not too expensive, unlike many of the higher-class inns, do not require an introduction to stay. When you do stay at a *ryokan*, there are several things to keep in mind:

The Police Box

Perhaps one of the reasons for Japan's generally crime-free streets is the very efficient network of branch police stations all over the country. More commonly know as "police boxes" (*koban* in Japanese), there are 1,250 of these miniature stations—manned by two or more officers twenty-four hours a day—in Tokyo Metropolitan area alone. In addition to patrolling their immediate areas by bicycle or on foot, police officers at the *koban* have detailed maps of their individual neighborhoods—indicating buildings, businesses, and residential houses—with which they are quick to give directions to anyone who asks. In addition to performing typical police functions, the *koban* also helps in such emergency situations as floods, typhoons, fire, electric power failure, lost children, and just about any other troubles that might occur in the local community. The police box will even lend those stranded enough money for transportation home. All police officers in Japan are required to practice either judo, kendo, or aikido (women officers are limited to the latter) until retiring from the police force, since the situations in which they may use their pistols and clubs are tightly restricted.

• Always remove your shoes before entering the house.

• Although slippers will be provided at the front entranceway, do not wear these into your tatami-floor room.

• The staff will lay futon mattresses out for you in your room at night, and in the morning—probably quite early—will come knocking on your door to clear them away.

• If meals are included—and in the nicer *ryokan* they invariably are—you will be served a Japanese dinner and breakfast the next morning in your room. (Although meal times are often predetermined, you might be asked what time you would like to eat.) The *ryokan* management plans the menu, varying with the season, but you may request substitutions if you call ahead.

• The entrance to the *ryokan* is customarily locked up at night, generally around 11:00 o'clock, so plan your evening activities accordingly.

Among Japanese *ryokan* are the traditional deluxe inns, which usually start from around ¥36,000 for two people. These distinguished establishments, many of which are steeped in history,

A tatami-mat room in a ryokan

maintain traditional Japanese values and customs. Private bathrooms are standard, in addition to a Japanese-style bath on the premises.

There are also the modern first-class *ryokan*, priced about the same as the deluxe inns, which combine Japanese tradition with Western convenience. Although the guest rooms and meals are Japanese-style, the structures of the buildings are modern concrete. These establishments will have bathing facilities similar to those of the traditional

English-Language Media

Four daily newspapers provide the best source of domestic and world news for the foreigner who cannot read Japanese. They are *The Japan Times*, *Asahi Evening News*, *Mainichi Daily News,* and *The Daily Yomiuri. The Japan Times* is the largest with a daily circulation of over 75,000. Other English-language newspapers include *The International Herald Tribune* and the *Asian Wall Street Journal.* The monthly *Tokyo Journal* is a good source for entertain-

ment information. Most of these publications are available at major hotels, Kinokuniya and Maruzen bookstores, and the kiosks in any of the major train stations. Major TV news stations offer bilingual broadcasts, and taped selections of CNN (Cable News Network), in English, are aired early in the morning and late at night on Channel 10. The U.S. Armed Services' Far Eastern Network (FEN) is the only exclusively English-language radio station, while others, such as J Wave, offer some English-language broadcasts.

Tokyoites dressed up for New Year's festivities

experience of traditional Japanese lifestyle at a fraction of the cost. Actually these are private homes, although guest rooms are often separate from the owner's dwellings. Guests are served home-cooked meals in a common room, sleep on futon in private rooms, and are provided with *yukata* (a light, cotton kimono) for the bath, but not necessarily towels. Prices run about ¥5,000 per person.

Western-style hotels add a 10 percent service charge to the bill, and *ryokan* 10 percent to 15 percent. In addition, there is also a 10 percent service tax collected by the Japanese government. Tipping, however, is non-existent. With the exception of some business hotels, some

deluxe *ryokan*.

Alternative bed-and-breakfast-and-dinner lodgings called *minshuku* offer an

---

National Holidays

January 1
New Year's Day (*Ganjitsu*)

January 15
Coming of Age Day (*Seijin no hi*)

February 11
National Foundation Day (*Kenkoku kinenbi*)

March 21*
Vernal Equinox Day (*Shunbun no hi*)

April 29
Arbor Day (*Midori no hi*)

May 3
Constitution Day (*Kenpo kinenbi*)

May 4
National Holiday (*Kokumin no kyujitsu*)

May 5
Children's Day (*Kodomo no hi*)

September 15
Respect for the Aged Day (*Keiro no hi*)

September 23*
Autumnal Equinox Day (*Shubun no hi*)

October 10
Sports Day (*Taiiku no hi*)

November 3
Culture Day (*Bunka no hi*)

November 23
Labor Thanksgiving Day (*Kinro kansha no hi*)

December 23
The Emperor's Birthday (*Tenno tanjobi*)

Business offices, schools, post offices, and other government services are closed on national holidays. Department stores and many shops and restaurants remain open, except on January 1. In addition to these days, many businesses close three to five days over the New Year season; part or all of Golden Week: April 29–May 5; and several days during *O-Bon*: mid-August.

*Dates are approximate

ryokan and most other lodgings in Japan will have refrigerators in the guest rooms stocked with beer, whiskey, soft drinks, bottled water, and snacks. There is a charge for these items, and the prices are usually listed on a menu somewhere in the room. In addition to normal broadcasts, cable TV is usually available for a fee. Also, many hotels and *ryokan* will call in a masseuse to the rooms of guests who so request. The fee is about ¥3,000 for a forty-minute massage.

Most hotels and *ryokan* are crowded during the spring (mid-March to end of May), summer (mid-July to end of August), autumn (October and November), and the New Year's holidays (December 29 to January 3). No matter when you are traveling, advance reservations are recommended, and essential during the busy seasons. Hotel and *ryokan* reservations can be made at any of the major train stations, and offices of most travel agents.

Hot springs (*onsen*) are the essence of the Japanese bath. Volcanic activity throughout the Japanese archipelago gives rise to thousands of *onsen*, many of

Jogging, Bicycling, and Swimming

Although jogging in Japan has never enjoyed the level of popularity it has in other countries, Tokyo does have its share of places to run. Among the best jogging routes are the three-mile course around the moat of the Imperial Palace, and Yoyogi Park's 1-1/2-mile course from Harajuku Station, around the NHK Broadcasting Center, Yoyogi National Stadium, and into the park itself.

Outside of Tokyo's major business districts and shopping centers, bicycling is allowed on the sidewalks, and along many roads there are even special cycling paths. Besides being a common way to commute from one's home to the nearest train station, bicycling is a popular form of recreation. Popular cycling routes include the two-mile course around the outer moat of the Imperial Palace. (Open Sundays only, 10:00 A.M.–5:00 P.M.; closed holidays.) You can borrow a bike free of charge from the police box in front of Otemon gate (entrance to the Palace Outer Garden, opposite the exit of Nijubashi-mae Subway Station).

Another scenic cycling spot is the tree-lined route around the Outer Garden of Meiji Shrine. To use a bike at no charge, inquire at the Meiji Jingu Gaien Cycling Center, near the Nihonseinen Kaikan Hall (Sundays and holidays only).

If you don't have access to a pool at your hotel, there are a number of public pools in Tokyo, but be prepared to line up to swim laps, as most will be crowded. Among these are the Tokyo Metropolitan Gymnasium Indoor Pool in Shibuya-ku (open all year around; 3408-6191), the Meiji Shrine indoor and outdoor pools (3403-3456; open June –September), and the indoor pool at the Minato-ku Sports Center (3452-4151) Alternatives, though much more costly, are hotel pools. Among those which allow visitors are the pools at the ANA Hotel Tokyo (outdoor), Century Hyatt (indoor), Keio Plaza (indoor and outdoor), New Otani (indoor and outdoor), Okura (indoor and outdoor), Shinagawa Prince (indoor), and Tokyo Prince (outdoor). (See "Selected First Class Hotels" for telephone numbers.)

which flow directly into the baths of *ryokan.* Since time immemorial, *onsen* have been valued by the Japanese for their medicinal purposes. Depending upon their mineral content—radium, iron, sulfur, etc.—these waters are

---

Selected First-Class Tokyo Hotels
S: single D: double

Akasaka
Akasaka Prince Hotel
   3234-1111   S: ¥24,000~   D: ¥32,000~
Akasaka Tokyu Hotel
   3580-2311   S: ¥19,000   D: ¥32,000~
ANA Hotel Tokyo
   3505-1111   S: ¥26,000   D: ¥34,000~
Capitol Tokyu Hotel
   3581-4511   S: ¥26,000   D: ¥37,500~
Hotel New Otani
   3265-1111   S: ¥25,500~   D: ¥33,500~

Ginza
Ginza Marunouchi Hotel
   3543-5431   S: ¥12,000~   D: ¥21,000~
Ginza Tokyu Hotel
   3541-2411   S: ¥18,000~   D: ¥29,800~
Hotel Seiyo Ginza
   3535-1111   D: ¥48,000~

Hibiya
Imperial Hotel
   3504-1111   D: ¥30,000~

Marunouchi/Otemachi
Hotel Grand Palace
   3264-1111   S: ¥17,000~   D: ¥29,000~
Palace Hotel
   3211-5211   S: ¥23,000~   D: ¥33,000~

Toranomon
Hotel Okura
   3582-0111   S: ¥32,000~   D: ¥40,000~

Roppongi
Roppongi Prince Hotel
   3587-1111   S: ¥19,500~   D: ¥23,500~

Shinagawa
Hotel Pacific Meridien Tokyo
   3445-6711   S: ¥22,000~   D: ¥25,000~
New Takanawa Prince Hotel
   3442-1111   S: ¥21,000   D: ¥29,000~
Takanawa Prince Hotel
   3447-1111   S: ¥19,000   D: ¥23,000~

Shinjuku
Hotel Century Hyatt
   3349-0111   S: ¥22,000~   D: ¥32,000~
Keio Plaza (Inter-Continental) Hotel
   3344-0111   S: ¥22,000~   D: ¥27,000~
Tokyo Hilton International
   3344-5111   S: ¥27,000~   D: ¥34,000~

Shiba
Tokyo Grand Hotel
   3454-0311   S: ¥12,500~   D: ¥16,000~
Tokyo Prince Hotel
   3432-1111   S: ¥24,000   D: ¥25,000~

Shirogane
Miyako Hotel Tokyo
   3447-3111   S: ¥18,000~   D: ¥30,000~

Ningyocho
Royal Park Hotel
   3667-1111   S: ¥21,000~   D: ¥30,000

Ochanomizu
Hilltop (Yamanoue) Hotel
   3293-2311   S: ¥15,000~   D: ¥22,000~

Ikebukuro
Hotel Metropolitan
   3980-1111   S: ¥16,000~   D: ¥21,000~

Mejiro
Four Seasons Hotel Chinzan-so, Tokyo
   3943-2222   S: ¥29,000   D: ¥33,000~

believed to have curative effects on a wide range of ailments, including skin disease, gout, and rheumatism.

Basic points to remember when enjoying an onsen are the same for any other communal bath at a Japanese inn. With towel in hand, wear the yukata bathrobe to the bath. (Both *yukata* and towel will be provided in your room. The small towel is for bathing, the large one for drying.) The door to the men's side is marked 男 , the women's 女 . Leave your *yukata* bathrobe in one of the baskets provided in the changing room, and you will be ready to enter the bathing room. Along the walls are faucets for hot and cold running water, little benches, and small tubs. Do all your washing here. The Japanese

The highlight of a stay at a Japanese inn: a dip in a rotenburo

Some Points of Japanese Etiquette

Although the Japanese do not generally expect the foreigner to understand the intricacies of Japanese etiquette, keeping the following pointers in mind will certainly help to make your stay in Japan more enjoyable.

• Instead of shaking hands, the Japanese custom is to bow. Westerners are not necessarily expected to return the courtesy when being introduced, as a handshake is certainly acceptable. (Japanese also bow when saying "thank you" and "goodbye," among other occasions.)
• When introduced in a business situation, proffer your business card.
• Before a meal, after cleaning your hands on the moist *o-shibori* (towel) provided for this hygienic custom, say "*Itadakimasu*" ("I will humbly receive").
• When someone pours you a drink (beer, sake, etc.) lift up your glass (or cup) to ac-

cept, then return the favor in similar fashion before drinking.
• After a meal it is polite to say "*gochisosama deshita.*"
• It is customary to bring a small gift (fresh fruit, cakes, cookies, etc.) when visiting someone's home.
• Before entering someone's home always remove your shoes, then say "*ojama shimasu*," which means, "Excuse me for interrupting you." If slippers are provided, never wear them into the bathroom, where special slippers for this purpose are provided. On the other hand, be sure not to wear the slippers which are for the bathroom into any other part of the house.
• Never use soap inside a Japanese bath (*o-furo*), as it is used for soaking. (Washing is done outside the bath.)
• The "Silver Seats," designated by blue and white seals over seats on trains and buses, are reserved for senior citizens and the handicapped.

bath is never used for washing, only for soaking. To melt away everyday stress, immerse yourself up to your neck in the hot water and simply relax.

Many *ryokan* located in isolated areas, such as the mountains or seaside, boast outdoor hotspring baths. Called *rotenburo*, these mineral spa pools are generally set in idyllic spots, where the natural scenery is as much a part of the bath experience as the soothing hot spring water itself. Most establishments maintain separate *rotenburo* for men and women, although communal bathing is not unheard of under the cover of darkness, not to mention the soothing effects of a few cups of warm sake, which might be imbibed while soaking.

Shinto and the Local Shrine

Shinto, or "Divine Way," is Japan's indigenous creed. Based on the providence of *kami* (gods), the laws of nature, and ancestor worship, Shinto is more a set of cultural rituals than it is a religion in the Western sense of the word—more a matter of being Japanese than a personal belief. And although Shinto has considerably less influence on daily life in comparison to Buddhism, its shrines are found in literally every local neighborhood in Tokyo, and indeed the entire nation. Dedicated to various popular deities connected to the livelihood and well-being of the local people, Tokyo's Shinto shrines, many of which date back to the Edo era, are the sites of ceremonies related to birth, coming of age, and weddings, as well as annual festivals celebrating spring, harvest, New Year, and so forth. The dances, processions, plays, music, and other spectacles at Shinto festivals serve to delight not only celebrants and onlookers, but also the deities, so that they will continue to bestow their blessings upon the local people.

On most days, however, a shrine is a tranquil place, with few pilgrims or guests to be seen. Admission is generally free, and everyone is welcome.

Pass through the *torii* gateway, which leads to the hall of worship. Often flanking the main entrance to the shrine grounds are pairs of Korean dogs, or archers, but if you see fox guardians you'll know that you are at an *Inari* shrine, where harvests are celebrated. Upon entering the grounds, feel free, but not obligated, to perform ablution by rinsing your hands and mouth at a stone basin filled with pure water. Many Japanese pay their respects at the hall of worship by standing before the cashbox and the long ropes handing from a gong. First they toss a coin in the box, sound the gong twice, bow deeply two times, clap their hands firmly twice, bow once again deeply and once lightly, before backing away from the altar to avoid turning their backs on the diety.

You might wish to purchase a written oracle or *omikuji* (sometimes available in English) or an amulet at the shrine office. After reading it, tie it on to a nearby tree branch (which will most likely be decorated with those belonging to other pilgrims) to invoke future blessings. Among the amulets are *ema*, small, wooden plaques with a picture, inscription, or both on one side, and a blank surface on the other to write your wishes.

An Introduction to Japanese Cuisine

*T*okyo has more restaurants than any other city in the world: making it truly an exciting and delicious culinary wonderland for anyone who is willing to step out and eat. With the vast numbers of dining establishments, Japanese restaurants tend to be very specialized, often serving only one type of food, which explains the overall high quality of dining in Japan on any level. All the better for the diner.

Only a few foods such as tempura or sushi have managed to make their way across the waters. Many first-timers to Japan will be amazed at the bewildering variety and scope that defines Japanese cuisine. We will cover just the basics, but there's lots more out there to taste and explore.

Unlike many other cuisines, Japanese cuisine is based on rice. Rice is not only the staple food here, but in Japanese, the word "rice" is the word for 'meal'; signifying its underlying importance. Therefore, rice signifies the end of a meal, generally preceded by an appetizer, a meat or fish dish, pickles and soup. Dessert, fresh seasonal fruit, is often only served at a top restaurant. Another essential element to the Japanese dining experience is the use of seasonal ingredients, especially fish and vegetables. This makes for always stimulating and new taste sensations, as most restaurants will change their menus on a seasonal, if not on a monthly, basis. Also, integral to the Japanese dining experience is the art of presentation, garnishing, and creative use of tableware. Japanese food is not only a feast for the tastebuds but also for the eyes.

Not delved into here is the delectable world of seasonal fish cooking such as sweetfish (*ayu*), eel (*unagi*), blowfish (*fugu*), and monkfish (*anko*). Also not to be missed is regional cooking of faraway spots within Japan—Tokyo has restaurants covering just about every major regional style of Japanese cooking.

Tempura

Choosing a restaurant in Tokyo is a painless procedure—the guidelines are simple. Most restaurants advertise in any number of ways, such as displaying plastic food models in the window. Other places will have a *noren* (short curtains) over the doorway—when these are hanging, the restaurant is open. Many places have English signs, or pictures of the type of specialty food served. Busy areas such as train stations, malls, and department stores always have a variety of eating spots located either in the basement or on the top floors of the building.

Hours of operation are fairly standard, although restaurants close earlier here than in the west. Lunch is served from 11:30 A.M. until 2:00 P.M., and dinner from 5:00 P.M. until 9:00 P.M. or 10:00 P.M., depending on the type of food. Closing days vary with each restaurant, so it pays to call in advance and reserve whenever possible. Most restaurants take yearly breaks at New Year's and during *O-Bon* festival in the summer (the third week of August).

Popular areas for dining in Tokyo include Ginza (expensive Japanese-style restaurants), Aoyama (lots of trendy foreign restaurants), Akasaka (the home of expensive exclusive dining establishments called *ryotei*), Roppongi (to many, the foreign ghetto in Tokyo—lots of fashionable foreign as well as traditional Japanese restaurants), Tsukiji (where the main fish market is located—go for sushi), Ueno *(shitamachi*-style traditional Japanese restaurants), Shinjuku, and Shibuya.

Most of the time, paying the bill is done at the front cashier as you leave. If the bill is over ¥5,000 per person, a six percent consumption tax and possibly ten percent service charge will be added. There is no tipping system in Japan. Always check beforehand to see if credit cards are accepted or not—Japan remains very much a cash society.

Set courses at lunch and dinner are popular in Japan. Usually several selections are offered each lunch and dinner, based on the number of dishes and in different price ranges. A la carte is generally available, often for a higher price, of course. Rice will be served along with tea and water as a matter of course in a Japanese restaurant, unless otherwise stated.

Here's a brief survey of some of the

Nambantei
friendly modern yakitori shop

4-5-6 Roppongi, Minato-ku, Tokyo
TELEPHONE: 3402-0606
HOURS: 5:00 P.M.–11:00 P.M. daily (also until 11:00 P.M. on holidays)
CREDIT: Major credit cards
NEAREST STATION: Roppongi (Hibiya Line)
PRICE: Courses ¥3,000/¥3,500

Yakitori (barbecued chicken and other goodies on a stick) is fun food to enjoy with drinks. Nambantei (there are several branches in the Roppongi and Shibuya areas) is the perfect place to gather with a group of friends and munch out. They are reasonably priced, with either set courses or à la carte menu to choose from. Sit at the counter and watch the jovial chefs grilling such morsels as asparagus wrapped in thin slices of pork (*asupara-maki*), their specialty of grilled miso-flavored beef, chicken wrapped in bacon or *shiso* (perilla leaf, Japan's answer to basil), and lots of vegetables like *shiitake* mushrooms, leeks, green peppers. Just about whatever can be grilled, Nambantei can deliver.

Tenmo
the way tempura should be

4-1-3 Nihonbashi-honcho, Chuo-ku, Tokyo
TELEPHONE: 3241-7035
HOURS: 12:00 Noon–2:00 P.M., 5:00 P.M.–8:00 P.M.
CLOSED: Saturday evenings, Sundays and holidays
CREDIT: No credit cards
NEAREST STATION: Shin-Nihonbashi (Sobu Line)
PRICE: Courses ¥6,000~ (lunch)/¥8,000~ (dinner)

Tenmo makes tempura the way it should be made but rarely is. Tucked away on a sidestreet in Nihonbashi, this thatched-roof restaurant, started in 1885, serves the most delicious tempura in town. It's very small: a counter for ten persons, and one tatami room also for ten persons. The best seats are at the counter, where you can watch the master at his craft. Lunch and dinner are the same price, and the only difference in the courses is the quantity, not the quality, so you never feel as if you're missing something. Tenmo uses only top-quality sesame oil and the freshest seasonal ingredients, and the batter is light and crusty, of the old school of tempura making.

Sukiyaki

styles of Japanese cuisine you can enjoy while in Tokyo.

Sushi/Sashimi: Sashimi is the most famous raw fish dish in Japan! *Nigiri-sushi* is what most eat in a sushi shop. Oblong-shaped seasoned rice is lightly touched with grated *wasabi* horseradish and topped off with a slice of the freshest

fish available. The eater lightly dips this into soy sauce (fish side first to avoid crumbly rice) and eats in one, or at most two bites. Use chopsticks or your fingers.

Tempura: Tempura is one of those dishes that can be either a culinary masterpiece of delicate lightness or an oily sodden mass. Tempura should be enjoyed at a top restaurant where the batter (*koromo*) reveals the shrimp, seafood, and vegetables at their best. Tempura can be eaten either with a dash of salt and a squeeze of lemon or dipped into a sauce called *tentsuyu*, to which grated daikon radish and ginger are added.

Yakitori: Skewered bits of chicken as well as seafood and vegetables are charcoal-broiled, some with a sweetened soy sauce glaze and others lightly salted. The

---

Tsukiji Tamura
traditional *kaiseki*

2-12-11 Tsukiji, Chuo-ku, Tokyo
TELEPHONE: 3541-2591
HOURS: 12:00 Noon–3:00 P.M., 5:30 P.M.–10:00 P.M.
CREDIT: Major credit cards
NEAREST STATION: Tsukiji (Hibiya Line)
PRICE: Courses ¥10,000 (lunch, from 5 people), ¥30,000 (dinner)

A history of over sixty years, a third-generation master, and proximity to the famed Tsukiji fish market ensure all Tsukiji Tamura's customers of the finest *kaiseki* meal. You have your choice of either Western-style seating on the first floor or private tatami-mat rooms on the second and third floors. Like any true *kaiseki* establishment, the emphasis is on the very best seasonal ingredients available, as well as beautiful and elegant presentation. The service is excellent and helpful. Reservations a must.

Iwashiya
haven for sardine lovers

7-2-12 Ginza, Chuo-ku, Tokyo
TELEPHONE: 3571-3000
HOURS: 12:00 Noon–2:00 P.M., 5:00 P.M.–9:00 P.M.
CLOSED: Sundays and holidays
CREDIT: Major credit cards
NEAREST STATION: Ginza (various lines)
PRICE: Courses ¥1,200 (lunch), ¥5,000~ (dinner)

Iwashiya, which has been around since before World War II, is enjoying a renaissance due to the current health-food boom. You have to love sardines, a highly underrated yet delicious fish. Here at Iwashiya you can enjoy sardines in every form from sashimi (eaten with grated ginger, not horseradish), in white miso soup, marinated, in tempura, and grilled. Enjoy the sardine memorabilia adorning the walls, making this truly a one-of-a-kind, entertaining establishment.

range of the *yakitori* depends only on the skill and creativity of the chef. This is perfect, affordable drinking food.

Shojin ryori: Often called monk's food, *shojin ryori* (no meat, fish, or eggs are used) has become the vegetarian's dream come true. With the recent gourmet and health-food booms, *shojin ryori* is an enduring, highly specialized cuisine.

Sukiyaki/Shabu shabu: Sukiyaki, the national dish, is a beefeater's delight. Thinly sliced pieces of top-grade beef and a variety of vegetables are simmered in an iron pan in a richly flavored sauce. Morsels are then dipped into a beaten raw egg and eaten with rice and pickles. *Shabu-shabu* is composed of extra-thin slices of beef briefly swirled into a boiling pot of water and then dipped into a variety of piquant and sweet sauces. Vegetables, and sometimes even noodles get the same treatment.

Noodles: Japan has a number of different types of cold and hot noodles. *Soba* is thin noodles made from buckwheat and wheat flour. *Udon* is made from wheat flour only, and while similar to spaghetti, is softer in texture. Summer noodles include dried varieties such as *somen* and *hiyamugi*. *Ramen* is Chinese-style noodles, yellow in appearance and often

---

Aragawa
meltingly tender Japanese beef

Hankyu Kotusha Bldg. Bl
3-3-9 Shinbashi, Minato-ku, Tokyo
TELEPHONE: 3591-8765
HOURS: 12:00 Noon–11:00 P.M.
CLOSED: Sundays and holidays
CREDIT: Major credit cards
NEAREST STATION: Shimbashi (JR line, Ginza Line),
Uchisaiwai-cho (Toei Mita Line)
PRICE: Sirloin or tenderloin steak ¥40,000~(set for two people), Sumiyaki dinner ¥45,000

It is said by many that Aragawa's steak is one of the best dining experiences to be had in Tokyo. The beef is very juicy and seasoned with just salt and pepper. The secret? Grilling the finest-quality domestic beef over the best charcoal in Japan, which comes from Kishu in Wakayama Prefecture. Before the grilling, cuts of meat are presented for your approval and you can select the piece you prefer. Accompaniments include specialities of the season offered in traditional *kaiseki* style. Unforgettable, and very expensive.

Echikatsu
generous portions of sukiyaki in a old-time traditional house

2-31-23 Yushima, Bunkyo-ku, Tokyo
TELEPHONE: 3811-5293, 3811-7417
HOURS: 5:00 P.M.–9:30 P.M.
CLOSED: Sundays and holidays
CREDIT: Major credit cards
NEAREST STATION: Hongo 3-chome (Marunouchi Line), Yushima (Chiyoda Line)
PRICE: Sukiyaki courses ¥6,000–¥11,000; Shabu-shabu courses ¥8,000

Echikatsu has been around since 1869 and knows not only how to serve great sukiyaki and *shabu-shabu*, but also how to welcome guests to this rambling, slightly ramshackle old Japanese house (featuring fifteen private rooms), located near famous Tokyo University. Their portions of Matsuzaka meat (from those pampered, massaged darlings) for their sukiyaki and *shabu-shabu* are generous for these days of minuscule portions. Winter or summer, Echikatsu is always packed with ravenous patrons. Reservations a must.

served in a rich soup made from pork or chicken bones. *Yaki-soba*, a luncher's delight, is stir-fried Chinese noodles mixed with vegetables and meat, mixed together with a thick, slightly sweet sauce.

Kaiseki: Comparable to French haute cuisine, *kaiseki* cuisine is the most refined and artistically presented food in Japan. Dish after dish is served, often just one mouthful, all based on seasonal delicacies. A whole manner of eating has developed with the evolution of *kaiseki*, with each course strictly adhered to. The most expensive cuisine in Japan.

Japanese-style Steak: Beer-fed and massaged, this prize Japanese beef from areas such as Matsuzaka, Kobe, and Omi is often served either *teppan-yaki* style, quickly sauteed in front of the customer, grilled on stones or charcoal-grilled *(sumiyaki)*. Taste the *shimofuri* (richly marbled meat) that literally melts in your mouth. This type of beef is ultra-expensive and need only be enjoyed in minuscule amounts due to its richness.

Fukuzushi
sushi at its most refined and modern

5-7-8 Roppongi, Minato-ku, Tokyo
TELEPHONE: 3402-4116
HOURS: 11:30 A.M.–2:00 P.M., 5:30 P.M.–11:00 P.M.
CLOSED: Sundays and holidays
CREDIT: Major credit cards
NEAREST STATION: Roppongi (Hibiya Line)
PRICE: Lunch course from ¥2,500, dinner course from ¥6,000/¥8,000/¥10,000

Eating sushi at Fukuzushi, considered by many to be one of Tokyo's top sushi spots, will be another unforgettable dining experience in Tokyo. You will sit at an immense counter made of one piece of *hinoki* (cypress) wood, with a dazzling display of today's catch (around twenty-five different items) spread out in front of you. Start off with a selection of sashimi, then move on to your favorite *nigiri* or *nori-maki* sushi, in which combinations of fish, vegetables and omelet slices are nestled in rice and rolled in crisp seaweed. Fukuzushi is well-known for choosing the best seasonal fish available; in winter, *hirame* (flounder); in autumn, *saba* (mackerel); and in summer, *karei* (sole). This is Tokyo-style sushi at its ultimate.

Genkai
chicken in a pot

5-5-1 Shinjuku, Shinjuku-ku, Tokyo
TELEPHONE: 3352-3101
HOURS: 12:00 Noon–10:00 P.M. daily
CREDIT: Major credit cards
NEAREST STATION: Shinjuku Gyoenmae (Marunouchi Line)
PRICE: Courses ¥7,000/¥9,000/¥11,000

Genkai is one of those restaurants that is a real delight to return to time and time again. Their *pièce de résistance* is chicken *mizutaki* (chicken in a pot), a soul-satisfying specialty of the Fukuoka region in Kyushu. Genkai's *mizutaki* is all chicken, with no vegetables in sight. Rich, yet not fatty-tasting, it's served with a diversity of condiments, including puréed garlic, grated ginger and chopped chives to add to the citron-scented dipping sauce. The chicken comes from their own farm in Fukushima and is also served in a number of other ways: from soft, white-meat sashimi to multi-flavored chicken tempura and salad. All of the seven tatami rooms are geared to privacy and superlative service.

Oden: A drinker's delight in the winter, *oden* is a hodgepodge stew composed of fish cakes, vegetables, and seafood simmered in a richly flavored fish stock (*dashi*). Eaten with a dab of fiery mustard and a flask of sake, it is the perfect inexpensive meal or snack.

It's true that Japan is no longer a budget country in which to travel in, but it is still possible to enjoy a large variety of foods in an economical manner.

For the budget traveler, stick to all-purpose restaurants called *shokudo*—these are inexpensive, yet surprisingly tasty and plentiful spots (serving a mixture of Japanese, Chinese, and Western dishes) found in department stores, shopping malls, arcades, and nearby big train stations. Foods that are usually low-priced include any type of noodle, *yakitori*,

---

Ukaichikutei
superb steak in a natural setting

2850 Minami Asakawa-machi, Hachioji-shi, Tokyo
TELEPHONE: (0426) 61-8419
HOURS 11:30 A.M.–10:30 P.M. (last order at 8:00 P.M.); Sundays & holidays, 11:00 A.M.–10:00 P.M.
CREDIT: Major credit cards
NEAREST STATION: Takaozan-guchi (Keio Line)
PRICE: Courses ¥6,800/¥8,300/¥9,500

Off the beaten track, Ukaichikutei not only serves scrumptious cuisine but is also one of the most visually beautiful restaurants in the whole Tokyo area. The sprawling restaurant, which was a guest house during the Edo era, is composed of many different buildings and tea houses tucked away in the foothills of Mt. Takao—Tokyo's answer to Mt. Fuji. Every private tatami room has a magnificent view of nature, such as a bamboo grove or a winding creek filled with carp. The cuisine is refined, highly sea-sonal *kaiseki*, with such extraordinary specialties as steak grilled on small *hibachi* (charcoal brazier) on fragrant oak leaves and served in a *miso*-flavored sauce. You will never taste such buttery, delicious steak anywhere else. Worth the trip, and considering the quality, the price is not unreasonable.

Unkai
quality hotel dining

ANA Hotel Tokyo (Ark Hills)
12-33 Akasaka 1-chome, Minato-ku, Tokyo
TELEPHONE: 3505-1111
HOURS: 7:00 A.M.–10:00 A.M., 11.30 A.M.–2:30 P.M., 5:00 P.M.–10:00 P.M. daily
CREDIT: Major credit cards
NEAREST STATION: Toranomon (Ginza Line), Kamiyacho (Hibiya Line)
PRICE: Kaiseki lunch ¥6,000/¥8,000/¥12,000; Kaiseki dinner ¥12,000–¥16,000/¥20,000; Shabu-shabu course ¥10,000; Tempura dinner ¥11,000/¥13,000

A beautiful tranquil Japanese garden, efficient service and an ideal location for the business traveler make Unkai a restaurant worth knowing about. Located between Roppongi and Akasaka and right next door to Suntory Hall, one of Tokyo's top concert halls, Unkai is open for breakfast, lunch, and dinner service. Take your pick of a variety of cuisines: Unkai serves *kaiseki*, tempura, and *shabu-shabu*, using choice paper-thin slices of Kobe beef cooked right at your table. Tables as well as tatami seating are available. Taking advantage of ANA's extensive transportation network, Unkai is able to provide its diners with wholly fresh ingredients of local origin.

oden, foods sold at *yatai* (street stalls), conveyor belt sushi, *yoshokuya* (Japanese-style Western food), *okonomiyaki* (a build-it-yourself Japanese-style pancake), and rice dishes such as curry rice. *Teishoku* or fixed plate (table d'hote) is the most economical way of ordering. It consists of an assortment of foods, including rice, soup and tea. This type of ordering can be done in most restaurants for lunch and dinner, as well as ordering a *bento* (boxed meal) instead of a set course, which is less expensive.

Dining well but not going broke can be achieved by having your main meal at lunch. Top restaurants offer set courses

An arrangement of sushi.

Yabu Soba
the most famous *soba* shop in Tokyo

2-10 Awajicho, Kanda, Chiyoda-ku, Tokyo
TELEPHONE: 3251-0287
HOURS: 11:30 A.M.–7:00 P.M.
CLOSED: Mondays
CREDIT: No credit cards
NEAREST STATION: Awajicho (Marunouchi Line), Ogawamachi (Toei Shinjuku Line)
PRICE: Tempura soba ¥1,500, Kamo namban ¥1,500, Anago namban ¥1,700

Yabu Soba is considered the ultimate, old-time *soba* shop. It's been around over 150 years and is now located in a newly built Japanese house in the old style in *shitamachi* (Tokyo's old downtown). The turn-over is rapid, as with many traditional older restaurants, but the service is friendly and your order is sung out to the kitchen, making it a noisy, welcoming place. The *soba* is some of the best in town. Specialties include soba topped with fried shrimp tempura and two soup-style *soba*: one with duck (*kamo*) and the other with conger eel (*anago*).

Yasuko
Japan's answer to pot-au-feu

5-4-6 Ginza, Chuo-ku, Tokyo
TELEPHONE: 3571-0621
HOURS: 4:00 P.M.–11:00 P.M.; Sundays and holidays 4:00 P.M.–10:00 P.M.
CLOSED: Sundays in August
CREDIT: No credit cards
NEAREST STATION: Ginza (Marunouchi Line, Hibiya Line), Yurakucho (JR Line)
PRICE: Oden (four kinds) ¥1,500; each type of oden ranges from ¥200 to ¥800 per serving; Sashimi from ¥1,400–¥2,200; Courses ¥6,000/¥7,000/¥7,500

The secret to perfect *oden* is long simmering and a good, rich, flavorful soup. Yasuko's soup is a lush-tasting concoction, just perfect for adding *oden* ingredients like *daikon* radish, *konnyaku* (devil's tongue jelly), tofu and a variety of fish-based dumplings. A dab of *karashi* (mustard) livens up the meltingly tender pieces of *oden*. Add a bowl of miso soup and rice, and you've got a complete meal. There's nothing like a bowl of *oden* and lots of saké to ward off the cold in the dead of winter.

for a lot less than at dinner. This way, even such delicacies as tempura and sushi can be savored. For medium-priced and expensive budgets, sukiyaki and *shabu shabu* should be tried.

An expensive meal includes *kaiseki* or a visit to a Japanese-style beef restaurant to savor *teppanyaki* or grilled steak, or a visit to a *ryotei* (which often needs an introduction by a regular).

What People Drink

Sake, after green tea, is the national drink. Brewed from fermented rice, this delicate tasting clear rice wine can be drunk either hot or cold. Mostly, it's served hot in a ceramic flask called a *tokkuri*. A true gourmet will drink it cold to enjoy the bouquet. Made in all parts of Japan, sake has no vintage years and is sold in two different grades (based on taxes, not quality), *ikkyu* (first class) and *nikkyu* (second class). (This classification will become obsolete in 1992 under a new tax law.) A reliable, yet slightly expensive brand is Ginjo.

Japanese beer is excellent. Some of the most famous breweries include Suntory, Kirin, Sapporo, and Asahi. Beer is enjoyed year-round, especially in the summer at beer gardens. Beer halls serve food and can be enjoyed at

---

Imari-tei
kaiseki at its most modern

Shimojima Bldg. 6F
3-5-25 Kita Aoyama, Minato-ku, Tokyo
TELEPHONE: 3478-5025
HOURS: 12:00 Noon–2:00 P.M., 5:30 P.M.–11:00 P.M.
CLOSED: Sundays
CREDIT: Major credit cards
NEAREST STATION: Omotesando (Ginza Line, Chiyoda Line, Hanzomon Line)
PRICE: Lunch course ¥8,000; Dinner course ¥12,000/¥15,000/¥18,000

A tiny jewel of a restaurant, with a sophisticated Western feeling, and pure *kaiseki* (Japanese haute cuisine) at its most innovative. The set courses change monthly, highlighting the choice ingredients of each season. There's room for only twenty persons, including counter seating, the best place in the house from which to view the chefs at work. Imari-tei is one of the few *kaiseki* restaurants to make approachable and enjoyable the mystery and allure of this painstakingly prepared food. The service is especially attentive and the atmosphere is relaxed.

Kiyota
top-class sushi in the heart of Tokyo

6-3-15 Ginza, Chuo-ku, Tokyo
TELEPHONE: 3572-4854
HOURS: 11:30 A.M.–8.00 P.M.
CLOSED: Sundays and holidays
CREDIT No credit cards
NEAREST STATION: Ginza (various lines)
PRICE: According to your order (no course offered)

The best way to enjoy a truly fine sushi restaurant is to leave yourself in the chef's hands. If you've got the money, just say to the chef, "*Tekito ni mitsukurotte kudasai*," which means "I leave the price and selection in your hands." Kiyota is an excellent place to do this in. The chef may look deceptively young, but his ability to select the choicest tuna and flounder in winter and abalone in summer will keep you coming back for more. Here are a few spcial words used only at sushi shops: *wasabi* horseradish becomes *namido* (tears), soy sauce becomes *murasaki* (purple), vinegared ginger becomes *gari*, and tea becomes *agari* (the end).

lunch and dinner.

Shochu, a distilled liquor made from rice or sweet potatoes, has recently attained great popularity. Although clear like sake, there's no comparison in taste—it's raw and very potent. *Chuhai*, a *shochu* cocktail, is also very popular.

Whiskey in Japan is often drunk as *mizuwari*—whiskey with water, or on the rocks (*onzarokku*). There are several brands to choose from, such as Suntory or Nikka.

There's also a large variety of soft drinks or juices, but always ask for 100 percent juice (*hyaku pacento* or *nama-jusu*) if you're thinking of the unsugared, natural variety.

Ocha, Japanese tea, can refer to any

Daigo
magical vegetarian cuisine

2-4-2 Atago, Minato-ku, Tokyo
TELEPHONE: 3431-0811
HOURS: 12:00 Noon–3:00 P.M. (last order 2:00 P.M.),
5:00 P.M.–9:00 P.M. (last order 8:00 P.M.)
CLOSED: Saturdays
CREDIT: Major credit cards
NEAREST STATION: Kamiyacho (Hibiya Line), Onarimon (Toei Mita Line)
PRICE: Courses ¥12,000 (lunch only)/¥14,000/¥16,000/¥18,000

Daigo's prices might astound you for vegetarian cooking, but this is *shojin-ryori*—Buddhist temple cooking—and Daigo is unequivocally haute cuisine in its outlook. The many-course meal begins with a personalized menu bearing your name. Daigo only has nine private tatami-matted rooms, and while the staff is small, the service is highly individualized. Draw back the *shoji* screens and feast your eyes on Daigo's exquisite Japanese garden. The restaurant was opened forty years ago at the request of nearby Seishoji Temple, which wanted to create a *shojin-ryori* restaurant. The manner of serving is *kaiseki* in style, with special attention paid both to the labor-intensive cooking and to its presentation in the beautiful ceramic dishes Daigo uses. You will dine and go away sated and smiling.

Tsukiji Suehiro
the finest Japanese beef

4-1-15 Tsukiji, Chuo-ku, Tokyo
TELEPHONE: 3542-3951
HOURS: 11:00 A.M.–10.00 P.M
CREDIT: Major credit cards
NEAREST STATION: Higashi-Ginza (Hibiya Line)
PRICE: Lunch course ¥3,000; Dinner course ¥5,000

Among the many kinds of Japanese cuisine, it is Japanese beef that is legendary worldwide for its fine taste. Suehiro was one of the first to serve this beef, opening their Ginza Steak House in 1933. In the more than half a century since then, the name Suehiro has become synonymous with the highest-quality Japanese beef, "*wagyu*" (Kobe beef, Matsuzaka beef, etc), grilled over charcoal into perfect steaks or thinly sliced into delicately flavored sukiyaki. Suehiro's restaurants are the most authentic places for the Japanese food that the whole world loves. The Tsukiji branch of Suehiro opened in 1964, and is every bit as good as the main restaurant. On the 8th floor of this building is The Teppanyaki Corner, where the skilled chef cooks your food in front of you at your table. If you want to hold a party, private rooms for 8–10 people are available.

number of different varieties, but generally means green tea. In *kaiseki* cuisine or in the tea ceremony, *matcha* (powdered green tea), a frothy, pleasantly bitter mixture, is served. Generally most people drink steeped green tea. The most famous types include *sencha*, which is served daily at restaurants; *bancha*, drunk daily at home; the least expensive, *hojicha* (roasted tea) or *mugicha* (barley tea), both refreshing brews served cold in the summer; and *gyokuro*, the most expensive steeped tea, enjoyed while eating Japanese sweets. In Japan, water or

Kamogawa
savoring blowfish

4-3-27 Akasaka, Minato-ku, Tokyo
TELEPHONE: 3583-3835
HOURS: 5:00 P.M.–11.00 P.M. (Sat. until 10.00 P.M.)
CLOSED: Sundays and holidays
CREDIT: Major credit cards
NEAREST STATION: Akasakamitsuke (Marunouchi Line, Ginza Line), Akasaka (Chiyoda Line)
PRICE: Fugu course ¥16,000 (September—April), Kaiseki course ¥10,000 (April—September)

Fugu (blowfish or globefish) is a much maligned (because of its poison) but highly prized delicacy that should be enjoyed during the right season (September to April), and Kamogawa is an excellent place to do this, with its polite service and cosy private tatami mat rooms. *Fugu* dinners usually follow a set pattern. First, start off with a glass of warm saké made aromatic by roasted *fugu* fin (called *hirezake*). Next, move on to one of the true Japanese culinary masterpieces called fugu-*sashi*: paper-thin slices of *fugu* sashimi set in the shape of a large flower and served with a dipping sauce of *ponzu*, a tart, citrusy soy sauce. The main dish is called *fugu-chiri*, a substantial and heartwarming stew made of pieces of *fugu* and lots of vegetables. The course finishes with the rice and beaten eggs added to the stew to make a gruel called *zosui*. To prepare *fugu*, chefs must obtain a national license which takes years of training.

Chotoku
noodles to classical music

1-10-5 Shibuya, Shibuya-ku, Tokyo
TELEPHONE: 3407-8891
HOURS: 11:30 A.M.–9.00 P.M.
CLOSED: Mondays
CREDIT: Major credit cards
NEAREST STATION: Shibuya(various lines)
PRICE: Chotoku nabe ¥6,600

This is the only *udon* noodle restaurant in town where classical music and Fauchon apple tea can be enjoyed, right along with sublime noodles. A single room with a choice of either tables and chairs or low-set tables on tatami, kimono-clad waitresses, a chef in the window rolling out the noodle dough, hand-painted tableware and choice pottery all create a sophisticated dining experience. Besides chewy tasty noodles, Chotoku's secret lies in using the best ingredients possible—the broth is composed of the best *kombu* seaweed, dried sardines, bonito, and *shiitake* mushrooms. The soup is almost smoky in flavor, and the specialty of the house is *sanuki udon*, a dish from the island of Shikoku that lies off Japan's main island. All the *udon* dishes are in either a *miso*-(soybean paste) or soy-based broth. Try the *nabeyaki udon* which is served in an iron pot, topped with tasty tempura prawns, fried in choice sesame oil with assorted vegetables.

tea, hot or cold, depending on the season, are always served gratis.

Mineral water is not always available in restaurants, but rest assured, all water in Japan is potable. Bars carry mineral water brands such as Mount Fuji or Rokko Mountains, as well as popular foreign brands.

Where People Drink

For the alcohol imbiber, there are many different spots to choose from. Japanese etiquette requires that if you are the host you serve your guests, always keeping their glasses full. They will return the favor. Remember if you wish to drink, raise your glass; if you don't wish to drink, put your hand over your glass. Casual and economical places to drink include *izakaya* (pubs), where inexpensive snacks and drinks can be had, or beer gardens, located on hotel and department store roofs (open only in the summer). There are literally thousands of little hole-in-the-wall bars, often seating just a few customers. Most of these places have a bottle-keep system, where you buy one bottle of your favorite liquor, which is then labeled with your name and kept for your private use. An *o-tsumami* (little appetizer) is served and you will be charged, whether you want it or not. These bars serve a variety of snacks. If you're really desperate, don't forget vending machines, selling beer, sake, wine, and whiskey.

Kissaten (coffee shops) serve coffee, tea, and a variety of snack foods.

Train Dining—A Japanese Specialty

The real secret to train dining (specifically on bullet and some limited express trains), lies not in the dining or buffet cars, but in the boxed lunches called *ekiben*. These wondrous boxes gives you a

Ekiben: *gourmet food for train travellers*

mini tour of Japan's regional specialties at a remarkably reasonable price. You don't even have to move from your seat—vendors constantly roam the train aisles selling *ekiben*, or you can buy at any train station.

It has been more than a century since *ekiben* were first sold in Japan, at Utsunomiya Station in Tochigi Prefecture. Today, there are close to 1,500 different varieties to choose from.

Ekiben, depending on the locality, are filled with such diverse foods as sushi, flavored rice, grilled Kobe beef, sweet rolled omelette, and Japanese-style pickles. The list goes on and on. They are always imaginatively boxed and wrapped. A few *ekiben* to savor includes "Toge no Kamameshi" (considered the top *ekiben* in Japan)—an earthenware pot filled with flavored rice mixed with various vegetables and teriyaki chicken, accompanied by pickles. "Genkikai" gets top marks for taste, presentation and ingenuity. Two layers of cedar boxes are filled with a variety of selections. For the oyster lover, Shamoji Kakimeshi features fried oysters from Hiroshima.

Some trains serve full course meals, but you should always inquire at the station before boarding. Usually, you can enjoy a perfectly ordinary and pricey meal in the dining car (with truly awful coffee) or pick up snacks and drinks in the buffet car.

Communicating

Communicating at a Japanese restaurant should not be difficult. You can try using English (speak slowly) or hand signs such as pointing to what another table has ordered. You can always lead a waiter out and point to the plastic food models in the window to show what you want. Here are a few handy phrases to use in restaurants.

Teishoku o kudasai. I'll have the set.
Omakase shimasu. I'll let you (the chef) decide. (Just tell them your budget, and the chef will decide the menu. This is very commonly done in high-class restaurants in Japan.)
Moriawase kudasai (at a sushi shop). Give me a selection.
Hai. Yes.
Iie. No.
Sumimasen, toire wa doko desu ka? Where's the bathroom?
Okanjo kudasai. The check please.

Akachochin *drinking spot under Yurakucho Station*

Ryoshusho o kudasai. A receipt please.
Itadakimasu (said before a meal).
Gochiso-sama (said after a meal). Thanks for a great meal.

Etiquette to Be Remembered

Nobody expects a first-timer to know the intricacies of Japanese dining manners, but there are a few things that, if remembered, will keep you in the good graces of just about any dining establishment and add greatly to your dining enjoyment.

*Learn how to use chopsticks! In Japan, these are the equivalent of a knife and fork. You can never truly enjoy Japanese food unless you can handle chopsticks (*hashi*). Eating with your hands is the worst possible manners (except with sushi).
*Never place your chopsticks upright in a bowl of rice. This is how food is offered to spirits of the dead.
*Rice is eaten plain, not topped with any sauce, unless indicated or served.
*Most Japanese meals, except for *nabe* (one-pot stews) are served individually, therefore if taking something from a communal plate, use the unused end of your chopsticks.
*Food is never passed from chopsticks to chopsticks. This is how bones after cremation are picked up.
* Napkins are usually not used during a Japanese meal. Instead, *o-shibori* (hot or cold damp towels) are given out, usually before dining and after something particularly messy is served. It is perfectly all right to spread your own handkerchief on your lap.
*Since rice and sake are made of the same ingredient, sake is not served after the rice course. Enjoy it with your appetizer and main dish.

Tokyo Restaurants

There are over 50,000 restaurants in Tokyo in an astonishing variety of styles to suit every budget. Don't overlook Tokyo's foreign restaurants if time allows, for many of them are truly of high quality. Some excellent restaurants in Tokyo's leading hotels are also worth considering, although they are more expensive than their equivalents outside. The following list provides a selection of restaurants in a general area, but be sure to check the exact location before leaving your hotel.

Roppongi

Antonio's (Italian)	3797-0388
Aux Six Arbres (nouvelle French)	3479-2888
Bengawan Solo (Indonesian)	3403-3031
Bodegon (Spanish)	3404-3430
Borsalino (Italian)	3583-4785
Double Axe (Greek)	3401-7384
Erawan (Thai)	3404-5741
Fukuzushi (sushi)	3402-4116
Ganga Palace (Indian)	3796-4477
Hassan (shabu-shabu)	3585-5388
Kisso (kaiseki)	3582-4191
Les Choux (classic French)	3452-5511
Nambantei (yakitori)	3402-0606
Seryna (sukiyaki, shabu-shabu)	3403-6211
Stockholm (Swedish)	3403-9046
Sushisei (sushi)	3401-0578
Takamura (kaiseki)	3585-6600
Tenshin No Ie (dim sum)	3478-8608
Toricho (yakitori)	3401-1827
Uoshin (tempura)	3403-1051
Victoria Station (steak and salad)	3479-4601

Akasaka

Akasaka Kamogawa (fugu)	3583-3835
Akasaka Shisen Hanten (Szechuan)	3263-9371
Chez Prisi (Swiss)	3224-9877
Daikokuya (tempura)	3844-1111
Kikuyoshi (sushi)	3585-2478
Los Platos (Spanish)	3583-4262
Mexico Lindo (Mexican)	3583-2095
Moti (Indian)	3582-3620
Tokusen Yoshinoya Akasaka (sukiyaki)	3586-0078
Tokyo Joe's (American)	3508-0325
Yushoku (sushi)	3583-0936
Zakuro (shabu-shabu)	3582-6841

Shinjuku

Ajisaijuku (kaiseki)	3225-7902
Bahn Thai (Thai)	3207-0068
Bombay (Indian)	3348-3725
Casa de Live (Spanish)	3368-0787
El Borracho (Mexican)	3354-7046
Le Coup Chou (classic French)	3348-1610
Rose de Sahara (African)	3379-6427
Suehiro (Japanese steak)	3356-4656
Tamagawa-zushi (sushi)	3200-1740
Tatsukichi (kushiage)	3341-9322
Tokaien (Korean)	3200-2924
Tsunahachi (tempura)	3352-1012

Shibuya

Chotoku (udon)	3407-8891
Heichinrou (Cantonese)	3464-7888
Madame Toki (nouvelle French)	3461-2263
Mao (teppanyaki, okonomi-yaki)	3409-3656
Osun Ghana House (Ghana)	3463-4734
Rheingau (German)	3406-4407
Samrat (Indian)	3496-4539
Sushi Bar (contemporary sushi)	3496-6333
Torikatsu (yakitori)	3461-0319
Tsunahachi (tempura)	3476-6059
Yagura (kushi-yaki)	3476-6021

Harajuku/Aoyama

Ghee (Indian)	3401-4023
Isshin (nouvelle French)	3401-7993
La Bohème (Italian)	3400-3406
La Mex (Mexican)	3470-1712
La Patata (Italian)	3403-9665
Le Chinois (Cantonese)	3403-3929
L'Orangerie (modern French)	3407-7461
Maisen (tonkatsu)	3470-0071
Mominoki House (natural foods)	3405-9144
Origa (sukiyaki)	3403-0527
Saatoku (unagi)	3400-3819

Ginza

Ashoka (Indian)	3572-2377
Gei-en (Korean)	3543-5154
L'Ecrin (classic French)	3561-9706
Tsukiji Suehiro (Japanese steak)	3542-3951
Ten-ichi (tempura)	3571-1949
Torigin (yakitori)	3571-3333
Tsukiji Edogin (sushi)	3543-4401

Nihonbashi

Hama (Japanese steak)	3573-0915
Inagiku (tempura)	3288-5501
Mimiu (udon)	3567-6571
Scott's (classic French)	3851-5481
Zakuro (sukiyaki, shabu-shabu)	3271-3791

Asakusa

Asakusa Chinya (sukiyaki, shabu-shabu)	3841-0010
Asakusa Miuraya (fugu)	3841-3151
Daikokuya (tempura)	3844-1111
Dojo Iidaya (dojo [loach])	3843-0881
Kuremutsu (traditional Japanese)	3842-0906
Miyako (sushi)	3844-0034
Otafuku (oden)	3871-2521
Sometaro (okonomi-yaki)	3844-9502

Shopping

The Japanese capital is the world's largest mercantile center. In fact, there is almost nothing that one cannot buy in Tokyo, which is home to about 240,000 shops, and 200 department stores. Japanese department stores satisfy virtually every consumer need, from fashion to furniture, prepared foods to imported wines, fine art to household appliances, round-trip air tickets and honeymoon reservations to wedding bouquets, and the list goes on and on, to include even new homes and grave sites. These meccas of consumerism, which maintain such high standards of service that they put to shame most of their Western counterparts, are also cultural centers where major art exhibitions—Cezanne, Van Gogh, European "Old Masters," old Edo, and ancient Egypt to name some—are commonplace. The Yurakucho branch of **Seibu** and the main branch of **Mitsukoshi** at Nihonbashi even have their own theaters. The top floors of Tokyo's department stores offer a wide range of good restaurants and cafes, while their roofs may maintain tennis courts, nurseries, and in the summertime, beer gardens.

In the capital's trendy districts are so-called fashion buildings, such as **Laforet** in Harajuku (see Harajuku section), **Fashion Community 109** in Shibuya (see Shibuya section), which can be described as crosses between department stores and fashion arcades. These ultra-modern buildings are filled with fancy boutiques offering top-name brands of both domestic and foreign designers.

Beneath many of Tokyo's busy business and shopping districts are underground shopping centers, which are bustling towns in their own rights, filled with a myriad of shops, including stylish clothing boutiques, book and record stores, jewelry shops, specialty food shops, restaurants, and bars. Tokyo's largest underground shopping centers are near the train stations of Shinjuku, Tokyo, and Shinbashi.

Harajuku, Takeshita Dori (Ave.)

Electronic Goods

Prices in Tokyo for Japanese electronic goods are not necessarily lower than discount stores in Hong Kong, Singapore, or even New York City, but what the Japanese capital does offer is tremendous variety and innovation. Some of the latest products often will not appear on overseas markets until months after they debut in Tokyo. The place to buy any kind of electrical equipment imaginable is Akihabara, where an estimated one-tenth of Japanese electronics sales take place. The electronic mecca of Japan, Akihabara has over 400 stores ranging from tiny shops selling electric tape, electronic cable, and batteries to giant discount department stores where each floor specializes in a different type of electronic product. Two big department stores are Ishimaru (3257-1200) and Yamagiwa

Discount electronics store in Akihabara

(3253-2111). The latter is Japan's top lighting specialty store, with literally thousands of different lamps to choose from. Some other big electric appliance stores are **Laox** (3253-7111), **Ono Den** (3253-3911), **Yamada Shomei** (3253-5161), **Tsukumo Denki** (3251-9851) and **Sato Musen** (3253-0597) which all have lots of video and TV equipment, including models that can receive multiple international broadcast systems.

You can expect a markdown of 20 to 40 percent at many of the shops in Akihabara, but bargains for less than half-price are not unheard of. In fact, Akihabara is one of the only places in Japan where price-haggling is acceptable. The smaller shops are usually more open to negotiation than the larger stores. But before going at it with the market-wise

Pocket T.V.'s in an Akihabara duty free shop

Tax-Free Shopping

In addition to the tax-free shops at Narita (and other international airports), major discount and department stores offer tax-free shopping for foreign tourists. Although you must pay the tax at the time of purchase, it will be refunded immediately when you present your passport at a special customer desk in the store. Duty-free items include those made of, or containing, precious metals and stones, pearls, tortoise shell, cloissone, furs, sporting guns, electronic goods, cameras and projectors, binoculars, watches, and tobacco pipes.

sales staff, you might want to visit several of them to compare prices. You may be lucky if your visit coincides with bargain sales offered during the summer or winter seasons, or at the end of the year.

In addition to those shops mentioned above, tax-free outlets for tourists are located in the **Teikoku Hotel Arcade** (3401-1111) in the Imperial Hotel. Here you can be sure of getting the correct voltage and number of cycles for use back home. Very near the Imperial Hotel is the **International Arcade** (3501-5775), where the tourist can find tax-free watches, more electronic goodies, pearls, cameras, pottery, kimono, and lots of colorful Japanese handicrafts. Be sure to bring your passport.

Several of the leading makers have showrooms in Tokyo where you can audition equipment at your leisure. Among these are the **Sony Showroom** (3573-2371) in the Sony Building in Ginza, and the **Pioneer Showroom** (3494-1111) in Meguro.

Cameras

The many discount camera shops in

Bargain hunting at a discount camera store

Shinjuku (see Shinjuku section) and Ikebukuro also offer good buys on electronic equipment, and of course, an extensive selection of cameras. **Yodobashi Camera** (3346-1010) in Shinjuku is the world's largest camera store. All 30,000 items stocked here are offered at a 20–50 percent discount. **Camera no Sakuraya** (3352-4711), also in Shinjuku, is a good place to check prices against competitor Yodobashi. **BIC Camera** (3988-0002) in Ikebukuro backs up its claim for being Japan's lowest priced camera shop by offering to refund the difference on any

Prices

Although many of the products purchased at any reputable store in Tokyo may seem expensive, the customer can be assured that quality will be a part of the bargain. This is largely due to Japanese consumers, who are perhaps the most fastidious in the world.

Taxes

In April 1989 the Diet approved a three-percent consumption tax levied on all expenditures, in spite of wide public opposition. While there is no tipping, a separate six-percent tax is added to hotel

bills over ¥10,000 and restaurant bills over ¥5,000.

Credit Cards

Although personal checks are not used in this country, major credit cards—MasterCard, American Express, Diners Club, Carte Blanche, and Visa—are generally honored by airlines, department stores, hotels, and many retail shops and restaurants. The majority of small, family-run shops and restaurants, however, will only accept cash, so you should be prepared.

World-famous Mikimoto pearls on the Ginza

Mouse alarms clocks to goldplated and fashion watches. The much more expensive **Wako** (3562-2111) is a division of the timepiece empire of Seiko, whose products are sold on the first floor of this most exclusive of Tokyo's department stores. The Wako clock tower, a Ginza landmark, is made famous by the Tokyo phrase "Meet me under the Wako clock." Another place in Ginza to shop for watches is **Tenshodo** (3562-0021), which actually began as an *inkan* (seal) maker back in 1879. Also known for its model trains, Tenshodo exports its own brand of steam locomotive models. Many of the discount camera shops in Shinjuku and Ikebukuro carry watches and clocks, although selections will be high-tech and contemporary, rather than elegant. A good selection of timepieces are also available at many of the department stores and jewelry shops.

product sold cheaper elsewhere. Other big-name discount camera stores include **Camera no Doi**, with shops in Shinjuku (3348-2242) and Shibuya (3464-5151). **Miyama Shokai** (3356-1841), also in Shinjuku, specializes in high-quality camera equipment for the professional. All of the shops mentioned above are open seven days a week.

Timepieces

Nihondo (3571-5511) in Ginza, established in 1941, has the largest selection of timepieces in Japan, ranging from Mickey

Pearls

One cannot speak of jewelry shops in Tokyo without mentioning the world-famous **Mikimoto Pearl** (3535-4611) in Ginza. This shop has been selling cultured pearls since 1899, six years after its

---

Flea Markets

Weather permitting, flea markets are held on the grounds of various shrines and temples around Tokyo. There is a wide variety of second-hand goods—some genuine antiques—to be found at these sales, which generally start early in the morning and last throughout the day. They are scheduled as follows:

First and fourth Sundays:
Togo Shrine (Harajuku)
Arai Yakushi Temple (a short walk from Arai Yakushimae Station, on the Seibu Shinjuku Line)

First Saturdays:
JR Iidabashi Station Building

Second Sunday:
Nogi Shrine (Akasaka)

Third Sunday:
Hanazono Shrine (Shinjuku)

Fourth Thursday and Friday:
Roppongi Roi Bldg (on the steps)

founder, Kokichi Mikimoto succeeded in culturing his first one. Mikimoto's motto "Best pearls, best jewelry, best service" describes aptly the quality—and prices—to be found by the visitor to this opulent and respected enclave. **Yonamine Pearl Gallery** (3402-4001) in Roppongi, owned by an American expatriate, caters to foreign businessmen buying for their wives back home, and offers to rebuy any pearls from dissatisfied customers. **Victor's Pearls** (3591-7785), in Hibiya, is another possible place to shop for pearls.

Boutiques

Japanese women are perhaps the most fashion-conscious in the world, attested to by the amazing amounts of money spent on clothing in Tokyo. American and European designer brands are easy to find, but they can be far more expensive than some of their internationally renowned Japanese counterparts. Department stores and so-called fashion buildings carry good selections of Japanese designs, and the leading designers also

One of Harajuku's many fashionable boutiques.

have their own shops. While most are made for the Japanese physique (sizes 7, 9 and 11), you will find many designs which are loose-fitting, and there is usually something to please most tastes. Most of the designers listed below also offer men's clothes and/or accessories.

Issey Miyake
3499-6476 (Minami Aoyama)

Emergencies

The emergency telephone numbers for the police and fire department are given below. Both will have English-speaking people on duty to help you. If you are calling from a public phone, lift up the receiver, push the red emergency button, and dial free of charge.
Police: 110
Fire and Ambulance: 119
Emergency hospitals where English is spoken are the following:

•International Catholic Hospital (Shinjuku area)

2-5-1 Nakaochiai, Shinjuku-ku
Telephone: 3951-1111

•St. Luke's International Hospital (Ginza area)
10-1 Akashi-cho, Chuo-ku
Telephone: 3541-5151

•Tokyo Medical and Surgical Clinic (Tokyo Tower area)
No. 32 Mori Bldg.
3-4-30 Shiba-koen, Minato-ku
Telephone: 3436-3028

Hanae Mori
3400-3301 (Omotesando)
Junko Koshino
3406-7370 (Minami Aoyama)
Junko Shimada
3463-2346 (Daikanyama)
Nichol (Mitsuhiro Matsuda)
5467-9111 (Gaienmae)
Kansai Yamamoto
3478-1958 (Harajuku)
Kenzo
(in Seibu department stores)
Y's (Yohji Yamamoto)
3409-6006 (Minami Aoyama)

Aoyama is home to internationally renowned designers.

For men, **Teijin Men's Shop** (3561-7519) in Ginza features a quality selection of traditional menswear, appealing to the gentrified look. **Hamilton Shirt Boutique** (3475-1971) in Kita Aoyama offers a discriminating selection of shirts—Issey Miyake, Ralph Lauren, and Hamilton—in large sizes. The **Y's** main Minami Aoyama shop offers a sporty and fun line of men's jackets and trousers, different from its austere selection of women's designs.

Noteworthy women's boutiques include **Alpha Cubic** (3499-4051) in Minami Aoyama, which features a wide selection of its own sophisticated, uptown, domestic and international brands, among them Boutique, Maison, and Blessed Damozel. This shop also carries the French brands Anne Marie Beretta and Renoma, and the Italian Guido Pasquali under license in Japan. In Ginza is **Tamaya International** (3563-4621). Established three centuries ago as a maker of sextants for nautical use, Tamaya has been specializing in stylish, well-tailored women's fashion since the 1970s. Imported lines include the likes of Yves St. Laurent, Chloe, and Renoma, but the company crest remains a sextant.

Japanese Baseball

Baseball and Sumo (Japanese wrestling), are Japan's most popular sports. Baseball has been played professionally in this country since 1936. Today there are two professional baseball leagues, the Pacific and the Central, consisting of six teams each. Annual pennant races consist of inter-league competition for 130 games between April and October. The pennant winners face each other for a best-of-seven-game Japan Series.

Each team is allowed to have two foreign players on its roster. In recent years, such major league stars as Warren Cromartie, Reggie Smith, Bob Horner, Bill Madlock, Cecil Fielder, and Vance Law have all played for Japanese teams. Despite such teams as the Seibu Lions (Pacific League), which has won many Japan Series in the last few years, it is Tokyo's Yomiuri Giants in the Central League that continues to be the most popular team, not only in the capital itself but throughout the country.

Gifts for kids of all ages: Kiddyland and Sanrio

Toys

Kiddyland (3409-3431) in Harajuku is a must for toy fans of any age. This toy department store is stocked from the basement to the fifth floor with toys, hobby accessories, party gear, greeting cards, and stationery, so allow plenty of time to browse, play, and maneuver you way past the hordes of other toy fanatics. **Sanrio Gallery** (3563-2731) in Ginza is the flagship store of Sanrio, the maker of Hello Kitty products and many other popular character toys. This store caters to little children, and as you enter, you'll be greeted by a talking tree in an enchanted forest. Another well-known toy shop in Ginza is **Hakuhin-kan Toy Park** (3571- 8008). Don't miss the salon on the fourth floor, where an exquisite collection of traditional Japanese and Western dolls is displayed. **Playthings** (3871-3186), in Roppongi's Axis building, and **Grand Papa** (3475-1388), in Aoyama, also have interesting gift possibilities for children of all ages.

Lacquer Ware and Ceramics

Traditionally, Japanese crafts, unlike those of many other cultures, fall in the realm of the fine arts. Of the hundreds of different kinds of Japanese crafts, lacquer ware and ceramics have the longest lineage. After being introduced from China around the seventh century, Japanese lacquer ware evolved its own distinct traditions with regional styles. Japanese lacquer ware is more durable than that of many other cultures because of its fine craftsmanship, with works of high quality able to withstand high humidity and extreme changes in temperature. The manufacturing process is a laborious one, requiring many coats of the refined sap of the Japanese sumac tree to arrive at a completely polished surface. Some of the more famous lacquer ware articles include Kyoto's *makie*, characterized by its graceful design and gold-and-silver-flaked surface. *Shunkei-nuri*, made in Gifu Prefecture, is noted for its thinly coated brownish surface. *Wajima-nuri* of Ishikawa Prefecture is popular today for its durability and utility.

While the earliest known examples of Japanese pottery date back ten thousand years, the craft did not develop into a fine art form until the Chinese and Korean influences of the thirteenth century. The tea ceremony and the art of flower arrangement influenced the artistic aspect of ceramics, and by the Edo Period (1603-1867) Japanese pottery had developed distinct styles and techniques, with nearly every local province producing its own unique ware. Today, Japan continues to be one of the world leaders in fine ceramics. Seto City on the outskirts of Nagoya is often considered the home of Japanese ceramics, with the term *seto-mono* (*Seto* ware) generic for all kinds of ceramics.

There are many lacquer ware shops among the prestigious traditional stores in the Nihonbashi district of Tokyo. One of these, **Heiando** (3272-2871), features lacquer ware of gorgeously polished finish. While products there can be quite expensive, this former purveyor to the Imperial Household maintains a tradition of very high quality. **Kuroeya** (3272-0948), another Nihonbashi lacquer ware shop was established in 1689. While most of the products featured there are of simpler style than those offered at Heiando, Kuroeya also claims the Imperial family among its customers. **Japan Craft Center** (3403-2460; closed Thursdays) in Minami Aoyama sells lacquer ware and other crafts from all over the country. If you are in the Akasaka area, visit **Inachu** (3582-4451), the Tokyo branch of a noted lacquer ware shop in Wajima on the Japan Sea coast, an area famous for lacquer ware craftsmanship.

The Ikebukuro branch of **Seibu** is noted for its excellent displays of ceramics, pottery, and other traditional crafts. **Imaemon** (3401-3441) in Minami Aoyama offers splendid ceramics which have been passed down through several generations since being offered to the Shogun and his retainers. **Koransha** (3543-0951) in Ginza stocks Arita ware, a style of porcelain named after its place of origin on the island of Kyushu. Arita porcelain is characterized by exquisite red glaze with gold, silver, and azure overglazes. Ancient Chinese ceramics can be bought at

A flea market at Nogi Shrine

Traditional antiques at the Oriental Bazaar

Kochukyo (3271-1835), located behind the south entrance of Takashimaya's Nihonbashi branch.

Antiques

There are many reputable antique shops in Tokyo. A number of them are located between Nezu Art Museum and Kinokuniya supermarket, on Kotto-dori ("Antique Road") in Minami Aoyama. **Morita Antiques**, for example, offers interesting items for the average purse. A short walking distance away are thirty antique shops in the **Antique Market** (3407-9363) in the basement of the Hanae Mori building in Omotesando. About two-thirds of these stores deal in Japanese antiques, the rest foreign. Nearby is the somewhat touristy **Oriental Bazaar** (3400-3933; closed Thursdays) in Harajuku, offering a wide selection of oriental antiques at reasonable prices. Popular items include lamp stands that are made from Japanese flower vases, folding screens, kimonos, *tansu* chests, and Buddhist figures. For a lengthy and enjoyable browse, try **Tokyo Ochanomizu Antique Hall** (3295-7112) in the Jimbocho section of Kanda, an area known for its wealth of second-hand and specialist book stores. The Antique Hall houses some fifty antique dealers, so that at any time the selection is vast, and often the prices are surprisingly reasonable.

For a wide selection of antique kimonos, look into **Hayashi Kimono** (3591-9826) in Yurakucho's International Arcade (see Ginza/Yurakucho section). Old Japanese furniture can be purchased at **Kurofune** (3479-1552) in Roppongi.

Traditional Souvenir Ideas

The following are some suggestions for traditional Japanese souvenirs, and places to buy them.

Japan Traditional Craft Center (3403-2460; open 10:00 A.M.–6:00 P.M.; closed Thursdays); one block from Gaienmae Station, at the large intersection. This excellent shop carries a wide selection of officially designated traditional crafts from all over Japan.

Bingo-ya (3202-8778; open 10:00 A.M.–7:00 P.M.; closed Mondays); in Wakamatsu-cho, Shinjuku-ku. This shop sells an abundance of folk crafts from all over Japan, including ceramics, fabrics, woodcrafts, lanterns, toys, dolls, drums, kites, glassware, lacquer ware, ironware, paper, and bamboo products. Take a bus (the No. 76, from the west side of Shinjuku Station) or a cab to the Kawada-cho bus stop. The shop is right there.

Beishu Co. (3572-1397; open 11:00 A.M.–7:00 P.M.; closed Sundays and holidays); in Ginza. This shop features a wide variety of Japanese dolls, starting at around ¥20,000, with some even selling for an astounding ¥2,500,000. Also available are figurines, masks, and folding fans.

Matsushita Associates, Inc. (3407-0279; open 9:30 A.M.–6:00 P.M.; closed Thursdays); near Omotesando Station. This shop sells woodblock prints, starting as low as ¥300. Reproductions can be purchased for around ¥2,500 and up, with old original works starting as low as ¥10,000.

Hanato (3841-6411; open 10:00 A.M.–8:30 P.M.; closed Tuesdays); ten minutes' walk from Tawaramachi Station. This shop offers many, many different kinds of Japanese paper lanterns.

Origami Kaikan (3811-4025; open 9:00 A.M.–5:00 P.M.; closed Sundays and holidays); five- or six-minute walk from Ochanomizu Station. This shop sells all kinds of paper used for *origami*, the Japanese art of paper folding, a fascinating pastime.

Sukeroku (3844-0577; open 10:00 A.M.–6:00 P.M.; closed Thursdays); near Senso-ji Temple in Asakusa. This traditional shop has been selling fine hand-crafted toys, dolls, and figurines since it first opened in 1860. Sukeroku is located at the end of the lane leading from the huge red Kaminarimon Gate to the main hall of Sensoji Temple in Asakusa. Called "Nakamise," this lane is lined on both sides with small shops selling a wide variety of traditional Japanese items, including articles worn with a kimono (sashes, elaborate hairpins, ribbons, petite purses, umbrellas, sandals, etc.), Japanese dolls, fans, ivory accessories, happi coats, imitation samurai swords of good quality (used in the martial arts practice of *iaido*), tortoiseshell accessories, rice crackers, and Japanese sweets.

● Clothing materials

Japanese	English
綿	COTTON
麻 { 亜 麻 / ラ ミ ー	LINEN / RAMIE

Japanese	English
絹	SILK
毛	WOOL

● Clothing sizes

MEN'S SHIRTS	JAPAN	36cm	37	38	39	40	41	42
	U.S. GREAT BRITAIN	14	14½	15	15½	16	16½	17
WOMEN'S DRESSES	JAPAN	7 号	9	11	13	16		
	U.S. GREAT BRITAIN	6	8	10	12	14	16	18

● Shoe sizes

MEN	JAPAN	22cm	24.5	25	25.5	26	27	
	U.S. GREAT BRITAIN	6	6½	7 ~ 7½	8	8½	9 ~ 9½	10 ~ 10½
	EUROPEAN	38	39	40	41	42	43	44
WOMEN	JAPAN	22cm	23	24	25	26		
	U.S. GREAT BRITAIN	4½	5½	6½	7½	8½	9½	10½
	EUROPEAN	36	37	38	39	40	41	42

Major Department Stores in Tokyo

Ginza/Yurakucho
- Matsuya (3567-1231)
  10:30 A.M.–7:30 P.M. Closed Tuesdays
- Matsuzakaya (3572-1111)
  10:30 A.M.–7:30 P.M. Closed Wednesdays
- Mitsukoshi (3562-1111)
  10:00 A.M.–7:30 P.M. Closed Mondays
- Printemps (3567-0077)
  10:00 A.M.–7:30 P.M. Closed Wednesdays
- Seibu (3286-0111)
  11:00 A.M.–8:00 P.M. Closed Tuesdays
- Hankyu (Sukiyabashi and Yurakucho branches) (3575-2231)
  10:30 A.M.–7:30 P.M. Closed Thursdays
- Wako (3562-2111)
  10:00 A.M.–5:30 P.M.; Saturdays until 6:00 P.M. Closed Sundays and holidays

Shinjuku
- Isetan (3352-1111)
  10:00 A.M.–7:30 P.M. Closed Wednesdays
- Odakyu (3342-1111)
  10:00 A.M.–7:30 P.M. Closed Tuesdays
- Keio (3342-2111)
  10:00 A.M.–7:00 P.M. Closed Thursdays
- Marui (3354-0101)
  11:00 A.M.–8:00 P.M. Closed two Wednesdays a month

- Mitsukoshi (3354-1111)
  10:00 A.M.–7:30 P.M. Closed Mondays

Nihonbashi
- Takashimaya (3211-4111)
  10:00 A.M.–7:00 P.M. Closed Wednesdays
- Mitsukoshi (3241-3311)
  10:00 A.M.–6:30 P.M. Closed Mondays
- Tokyu (3273-3111)
  10:00 A.M.–7:30 P.M. Closed Thursdays

Shibuya
- Seibu (3462-0111)
  11:00 A.M.–8:00 P.M. Closed Wednesdays
- Tokyu Main Store (3477-3111)
  10:00 A.M.–7:30 P.M. Closed Tuesdays
- Tokyu Toyoko Branch (3477-3111)
  10:00 A.M.–7:30 P.M. Closed Thursdays
- Marui (3464-0101)
  11:00 A.M.–8:00 P.M. Closed one or two Wednesdays a month

Ikebukuro
- Seibu (3981-0111)
  10:00 A.M.–8:00 P.M. Closed Tuesdays
- Tobu (3981-2211)
  10:00 A.M.–8:00 P.M. Closed Wednesdays
- Mitsukoshi (3987-1111)
  10:30 A.M.–7:30 P.M. Closed Mondays

Tokyo Nightlife

Many Tokyo districts have unique personalities by day, which transform into nocturnal arenas of epicurean delight after dark. The neon-soaked girly bars of Shinjuku's Kabuki-cho, the high-class hostess clubs of Ginza, the chic cabarets and nightclubs of Akasaka, Roppongi's screaming discos and bars that stay open until dawn, Shibuya's youth-filled beer halls and pubs, and Ikebukuro's Shinjuku-style cheap thrills all contribute to the versatile energy of what is Tokyo after dark.

There are a few points, however, which the visitor should heed. Like so much else in the Japanese capital, entertainment at night can be very costly. Many of the exclusive night spots are frequented mostly by white collar workers with generous expense accounts. The visitor is strongly advised not to wander inside a bar he or she is unsure of, unless escorted by one who is familiar with that particular establishment. Depending on the neighborhood, the tab for just a drink or two might very well exceed that for a full-course dinner at a high-class restaurant. There is no limit to the cost of drinking for a couple of hours in the hostess clubs of Ginza, Akasaka, Shinjuku, and Roppongi, where the bill can add up to more than $300 per person. Nor is it recommended that the visitor wander alone into the X-rated shops (i.e., massage parlors, bathhouses, girly bars, etc.) of Shinjuku, Ikebukuro, Shibuya, and the like. Many of these places are run by *yakuza* (Japanese gangsters), who are known to charge much more than the originally stated prices.

But for the most part, a night out in Tokyo hardly warrants much caution. Aside from the types of places mentioned above, most drinking establishments and

ANA Hotel's Da Vinci bar

other night spots around the capital offer good, honest service at posted prices. Below are some suggestions:

Nomiya, or "Drinking Establishments"

Bars, nightclubs, pubs, and any other place to drink in Japan can be labeled *nomiya*, or "drinking establishment." Since the Japanese are accustomed to eating while drinking, most pubs offer extensive menus of prepared food, in addition to various types of alcoholic beverages. Usually inexpensive are the *akachochin*, or "red lantern" *nomiya*, thus called for the red lantern(s) hanging near the entranceway. In addition to Japanese sake, *akachochin* serve beer, whisky, and usually *shochu* (a distilled spirit most often made from potatoes, buckwheat, barley, or rice). Some specialize in one particular type of cuisine, among which *yakitori*, or "skewered chicken," is very common. But most *akachochin* offer wide selections of prepared food, both Japanese and Western, to satisfy a variety of palates. These pubs in Tokyo start getting crowded after office hours (from around 6:00 P.M.), with most

Tokyo beer halls are popular gathering places

staying open until midnight or later.

The Japanese love of good brew is attested to by the great popularity of Tokyo's beer halls and beer gardens. The Japanese, in fact, drank an average of 6 1/2 gallons (24 liters) of beer per person between June and August 1990, pushing beer sales to a record 607,200 gallons (2.18 million liters). Beer halls offer a variety of brews on draught or in the bottle, and an extensive food menu at reasonable prices. **Lion Beer Hall** in Ginza (3571-2590), established in 1934, is famous for its high ceiling and glass mosaic decoration. The chic Asahi beerhall in Asakusa, dubbed **La Flamme d'Or** (5608-5381), features French-style cuisine. Situated along the Sumida River near Azumabashi bridge, next door to the headquarters of

A Note About Earthquakes and Typhoons

It is a scientific fact that major quakes occur about every sixty years in Japan. As there has not been a big earthquake on the archipelago since that which devastated Tokyo in 1923, seismologists predict one of dangerous magnitude in the near future. Minor tremors occur frequently, and Tokyoites are understandably well informed—and calm—about them. If a quake should strike be sure to do the following:

If you are inside, stay there. Extinguish all flames, including cigarettes and heaters, as strong earthquakes often cause fires. If you are in a place where gas is used, close the main valve. Open a door or window for ventilation, and to be sure that you have a way out in case of fire. Get under a table, desk, or bed to protect yourself from falling objects.

After the tremor subsides, turn on the television (NHK) or radio (FEN, in English) for updates.

If you are outside, go into the nearest building (avoid train and subway stations, freestanding walls, and glass windows), or wide open space. Parks, athletic fields, playgrounds, and other such places will become evacuation sites. Stay away from the ocean, as tidal waves are possible where the sea is level, and landslides where it is not.

If you happen to be visiting Tokyo between midsummer and late September (occasionally as late as mid-October), you might encounter a typhoon. Although these violent storms can be dangerous (by definition a typhoon has winds exceeding 117 mph), adequate storm warnings are always given. Even the most powerful typhoons will usually subside in a matter of hours.

Asahi Breweries, Ltd., the building is immediately recognizable by the golden flame on its roof (some claim it looks more like a giant carrot). The design of the avant-garde interior was based on the architect's image, in a dream, of the inside of a submarine. The **Kirin City** (main branch; 3408-6581) in Roppongi (there are fifteen others around Tokyo) always pours draught beer slowly to ensure just the right head, at the best temperature. Other popular beer bars include **Beer Bar 25** (3505-5525) in Roppongi and **Hofbrauhaus Munchen** (3207-7591) in Shinjuku.

If you are visiting Tokyo during the summer months, you might want to try one of the many beer gardens, most of which are located high above the city on the roofs of department stores, hotels and other buildings. For a down-to-earth (literally) and idyllic retreat from the concrete city, visit the Japanese-style **Gajoen Green Beer Garden** (3491-4111) in Shimomeguro.

Live Music

Of the many types of Western music

Pit Inn, where R & B and reggae first hit Tokyo

that have permeated Japanese culture, perhaps jazz is the most popular. In fact, some American visitors claim that live jazz is more readily available in Tokyo than back home. A must for any jazz fan is **Blue Note Tokyo** (3407-5781) near Roppongi, which is a replica of the world-famous club by the same name in New York City. Top-class musicians from the United States perform here regularly (entrance charge ¥8,000—¥12,000; open 6:00 P.M.–2:00 A.M., except Sunday). Also in Roppongi is **Birdland** (3478-3456), whose regular band specializes in 1940s and 1950s jazz standards (cover charge ¥3,500; open daily, 7:00 P.M.–1:00 A.M., Fridays and Saturdays 8:30 P.M.–1:00 A.M.). **Roppongi Pit Inn** (3585-1063), where such Japanese greats as Watanabe Sadao and Kikuchi Masaki got started, also features blues and reggae (cover charge Depends; open daily, 6:30 P.M.–10:00 P.M.). For a more refined atmosphere, Roppongi's **Satindoll** (3401-3080) combines live jazz with French cuisine (cover charge ¥1,500 and up; open daily, 5:30 P.M.–midnight). To mix French food with jazz, go to **Satindoll** in Roppongi (3401-3080), where visit-

Blue Note Tokyo—Japan's premier jazz spot

ing foreign musicians perform several times a year (cover charge ¥1,300~; open daily, 5:30 P.M.–midnight).

For reggae, the usually crowded **Hot Corocket** (3583-9409) in Roppongi has a resident Jamaican band (the cover charge, cheaper for ladies, includes two drinks; open Monday–Saturday, 7:00 P.M.–3:00 A.M., closed Sundays).

Karaoke

If hamming it up is your thing, you might want to experience one of the countless karaoke, or "sing along" bars, where the customers do just that. Young and old, male and female, patrons shed their daytime inhibitions (usually after a few drinks) and sing along into a microphone to a pre-taped musical accompaniment of their favorite tunes. The lyrics are provided in a songbook, or in many

A drink and a song at a karaoke bar

Churches and Religious Organizations

The following is a guide to selected religious services and centers in Tokyo for the foreign visitor:

•**Franciscan Chapel Center** (Roppongi)
Telephone: 3401-2141
Monday–Saturday: 8:00 A.M., 6:00 P.M.
Sunday services: 8:00 A.M.
                              10:00 A.M.
                              12:00 Noon
                              6:00 P.M.

•**Tokyo Union Church** (Omotesando)
Telephone: 3400-0047
Sunday services: 8:30 A.M.
                              11:00 A.M.

•**Tokyo Baptist** (Daikanyama)
Telephone: 3461-8425
Sunday services: 9:30 A.M., 10:50 A.M.
                              6:00 P.M.

•**The Jewish Community Center** (Hiroo)
(offers kosher food)
Telephone: 3400-2559
Sabbath services:
Fridays   6:30 P.M.
Saturdays   9:30 A.M.

•**The Orthodox Church in Japan**
(Ochanomizu) (Russian Orthodox)
Telephone: 3291-1885
Services:
Saturdays   6:00 P.M.
Sundays   10:00 A.M.

•**Arabic Islamic Institute** (Roppongi)
Telephone: 3404-6411
Mosque prayers on Fridays: 12:00 Noon

cases on a TV screen through laser disk, with an image—maybe an idyllic scene—supposedly providing inspiration to the singer. So-called snack bars (where the bill includes a nominal table charge for a small appetizer which is automatically served to all customers), and hostess bars are the most common settings for karaoke.

Discos

Most of Tokyo's better discos are in the ¥4,000–¥5,000 range, with entrance fees for men usually costing ¥500 more than for women. The atmosphere will be aptly luxurious—drinks and food are often included in the price of admission, and to maintain a level of respectability, men usually are not permitted to enter without a female companion. Suggested places for dancing, most of which attract a large foreign crowd, are:

• **Lexington Queen** (3401-1661; open

Feel the disco beat in the center of Tokyo

Estimated Expenses: First Class

Lodgings	¥25,000/person (twin room)
Breakfast	¥2,500 (hotel coffee shop)
Lunch	¥5,000 (set course)
Dinner	¥10,000 (set course)
Transportation	¥3,500 (taxi and subway)
Entertainment	¥10,000 (medium-priced seats at Kabuki-za)
Total:	¥56,000 ($509) ($1.00 = ¥110)

It is possible to cut the above expenses by two-thirds if you eat at restaurants frequented by the average Japanese, rely on public transportation, lodge at a budget hotel, and see kabuki at the National Theater.

nightly until 4:00 A.M.}: This established Roppongi disco has been patronized by such big-name entertainers as Stevie Wonder, Rod Stewart, Sly Stallone, Duran Duran, and Queen. Foreign models are admitted free of charge, and sushi is included in the price of admission.

•**Buzz** (3470-6391; open nightly until 5:00 A.M.) This adult-oriented discotheque, located in what is sometimes called Roppongi's "Disco Building," is a favorite among the embassy crowd and foreign journalists. The music is never so loud as to impede conversation, and there is a comfortable, softly lit lounge for those who prefer talking to dancing.

•**Radio City Hibiya** (3503-3675; open 6:00 P.M.–midnight): Futuristic, fantastic sound and light effects. Located in Toho Twin Tower Building near Hibiya Subway Station.

•**Velfarre** (3402-8000; open 6:00 P.M.–midnight): A smart disco (with some dress restrictions) with a great atmosphere, near exit 4B of Roppongi Subway Station.

Theaters

Among Tokyo's numerous contemporary theaters, foreign fans of modern drama

Huge Japanese wrestlers battle it out in a sumo contest

who are in the market for something different might enjoy **Tokyo Takarazuka Gekijo** (3591-1711) in Hibiya. This theater's unique *Kagekidan* troupe is, in a sense, the inverse of kabuki; its all-women cast play both male and female roles. The performances—Harlequin Romance-type fantasy—feature colorful settings and costumes. *Kagekidan* performances start Monday through Saturday at 1:00 P.M. and 5:30 P.M., and on Sunday at 11:00 A.M. and 3:30 P.M., with admission ranging from ¥1,100 to ¥5,300.

For traditional Japanese drama visit the **National Theater of Japan** near Nagatacho Station (see the Nagatacho section). **The Shinjuku Koma Theater** (3202-8111), famous for its revolving stage, features leading contemporary Japanese plays and popular singers.

Underground and Artistic Cinemas

Aficionados of avant-garde film, both Japanese and foreign, may appreciate **Image Forum** (3358-1983), just a minute's

A dramatic scene from the Kabuki

walk from Yotsuya-sanchome Station on the Marunouchi Subway Line. Underground movies featured here include experimental works, short films, and documentaries, and are shown Thursdays through Saturdays, from 5:00 P.M. and 7:00 P.M., and on Sundays and national holidays from 1:00 P.M. and 3:00 P.M.

Tokyo also has a number of independent cinemas which specialize in artistic European, American, Asian, and Russian films. Below are some selections:

- **Ginza Theatre Seiyu** (3535-6000; Ginza)
- **Cinema Square Tokyu** (3232-9274; Shinjuku)
- **Haiyu-za Cinema Ten** (3401-4073; Roppongi)
- **Kino Aoyama** (5485-2890; Aoyama)
- **Eurospace** (3461-0211; Shibuya)

Sumo

Sumo is Japan's national sport and oldest martial art. This 2000-year-old form of wrestling began as a sacred Shinto rite, and many of its ancient rituals are still practiced today. One of these—the barring of women from entering the clay fighting ring—recently caused an uproar when a female chief cabinet secretary was not permitted into the ring to present the Prime Minister's Cup to a tournament champion. The Emperor customarily attends at least one day of matches in Tokyo annually, a tradition historians believe began in A.D. 100.

The object of sumo is to throw one's opponent so that some part of his body, other than the soles of his feet, touches the ground, or force him out of the fifteen feet (4.55 meter) ring, using any combination of some seventy-odd techniques. Six annual tournaments, each lasting fifteen days, provide thirty-eight of the highest ranking *Makuuchi* Division wrestlers an opportunity to fight one match a day. The wrestler with the most victories on the closing fifteenth day is the tournament champion, with sudden death matches held in case of ties. The **Kokugikan** (3623-5111) in Ryogoku, just north of Ryogoku Station, is home to three tournaments (January, May, September), with the remaining three held once each in Nagoya, Fukuoka, and Osaka. Bench seats, located high up in the back, cost ¥1,500; second-level seats are ¥2,300 to ¥7,000; box seats, which include lunch and sake, run ¥7,500 to ¥9,500, but are very difficult to come by. Tickets go on sale about three weeks in advance, and can be purchased directly at the Kokugikan or from various ticket agencies around Tokyo. Matches begin at noon, but the *Makuuchi* wrestlers don't start fighting until 4:00 P.M. NHK (Channel 1) televises the matches from 4:00 to 6:00 P.M. every afternoon during the fifteen-day period of each tournament.

Near the main entrance of the Kokugikan is the **Sumo Museum** (3622-0366; open 9:30 A.M.–4:30 P.M.; closed Sundays and holidays), which exhibits a variety of sumo-related items. The Sumo Photographic Reference Center (3631-2150; open 10:00 A.M.–5:00 P.M. every Tuesdays, and daily during the January, May and September tournaments) features some 60,000 sumo-related photos, including famous wrestlers of the past, and the Ryogoku sumo quarter in the Edo Period. Also on display are handprints of famous wrestlers.

Sightseeing

So numerous are the cultural landmarks
and facilities in the Japanese capital, it
would be impossible to cover more than
just a small fraction of them here.
Accordingly, we have depended on the
very history of the city to help us with
our choices, which center on the Imperial
Palace, formerly the castle of the Tokugawa Shoguns, and around the Sumida
River, along whose banks sprang forth the
culture of the common people of Edo.
Also we have provided a short guide to
other suggested sightseeing spots in
Tokyo, including parks, museums,
shrines, and temples.

Imperial Palace and Grounds

Any tour of Tokyo should include a stroll around the Imperial Palace, which occupies the geographic and historic center of the Japanese capital. Easily accessible from both Tokyo and Otemachi Stations, and surrounded by exquisite gardens, forbidding stone walls, and deep moats, the palace was formerly the site of Edo Castle, the powerful stronghold of the Tokugawa Shogunate for over two and a half centuries. Shortly after the Meiji Restoration in 1868, the Emperor took up residence here, and in 1889 constructed a new palace, which was destroyed by air raids during World War II. After the Meiji era, two successive emperors lived at the palace, while the present Emperor Akihito (enthroned November 1990) currently resides within the grounds of the Akasaka Detached Palace.

The present Imperial Palace (rebuilt after the war) and grounds cover a vast area of 280 acres. Its remaining moat consists of three waterways, which have long been home to swans and carp. Entrance to the inner grounds of the Imperial Palace is tightly restricted, but there are several sections of the palace grounds which are open to the public throughout most of the year. Among these are Kitanomaru Koen Park, Chidorigafuchi Water Park, the East Garden, and the Imperial Palace Plaza.

Kitanomaru Koen Park, formerly the domain of the Imperial Guard, boasts exquisite gardens, first-class museums, and grand auditoriums. Among this park's museums is the **National Museum of Modern Art** (3214-2561; open 10:00 A.M.—5:00 P.M.; closed Mondays; admission: ¥1,000) which houses over 3,000 works of what is considered Japan's finest modern art collection. In the same

Jogging around the Imperial Palace

park is another national museum of modern art, which is called the **Tokyo Crafts Gallery** (3211-7781; open 10:00 A.M.–5:00 P.M.; closed Mondays; admission:¥400). Its Gothic-style red brick building (1910), representative of Meiji-era architecture, was formerly the headquarters of the Imperial Palace Guard. Today this museum boasts the finest collection of modern crafts in the country. Also in Kitanomaru Koen is the pentagonal **Science and Technology Museum** (3212-8471; Open 9:30 A.M.–4:50 P.M.; open daily.) Features here include ATOMA, an atomic robot which walks and talks, and a 360-degree movie screen. The **Budokan**, another Kitanomaru Koen attraction, is an enormous octagonal hall originally built in 1964 to host martial arts events for the Tokyo Olympics, but which is now world-famous as a venue for rock concerts. Leading into the park, near the Budokan, is Tayasumaru Gate, which also serves as an entrance to the outer precincts of Yasukuni Shrine.

Chidorigafuchi Water Park, another section of the Imperial Palace open to the public, is situated along the west side of Hanzo Moat, just north of Hanzomon gate. Migratory birds enhance the beauty of this oblong park, which in spring is famous for its beautiful cherry blossoms. Near the moat is the **Tomb of the Unknown Soldier**, which contains the remains of some 90,000 victims of combat.

Also open to the public is **Kokyo Higashi Gyoen**, or Imperial Palace East Garden, which contains the remains of the inner fortress of Edo Castle. Some 260 varieties of trees are planted in these grounds, accessible through three of the gates which led into Edo Castle. These are Otemon, formerly the main entrance to Edo Castle; Kitakibashimon, which was the entrance to the castle tower; and Hirakawamon, which served as both the main entrance to the third fortress of the old castle, and side exit for women of the Shogun's inner chambers. The East Garden is open 9:00 A.M.–4:00 P.M.; closed Mondays, Fridays, and on special state occasions.

At the main approach to the Imperial Palace is **Nijubashi**, or "Double Bridge," a site not to be missed. As its name may indicate, Nijubashi consists of two fairly modern bridges; the double-arched structure in the foreground is made of stone, the other iron. Fushimi Tower looms across the moat behind the bridges, its white walls blending exquisitely with its black tile roof. The contrast of the Western-style stone bridge reflecting in the moat, and the traditional castle tower rising majestically in the background, produces one of Tokyo's most picturesque scenes. It was through the Nijubashi Gate that the funeral procession for the late Emperor Showa (1901–1989; enthroned 1926) passed, as a sea of mourners stood in silent reverence one cold, rainy February morning.

The best view of Nijubashi is from the Imperial Palace Plaza, another section of the Palace open to the public. One of the few wide-open spaces in Tokyo, the plaza's lawns, raked gravel area, and pine thickets make it the perfect respite from the business of surrounding Tokyo.

Yasukuni Shrine

West of Kitanomaru Koen park is **Yasukuni Shrine** (3261-8326; main hall open 9:00 A.M.–5:00 P.M., shrine always open), a ten-minute walk from Kudanshita Subway Station, dedicated to those who died fighting for Japan from around the Meiji Restoration (1868) to the end of World War II. Some 2.5 million souls are enshrined at Yasukuni, including such Class A war criminals as Tojo Hideki (executed by the Allies in 1948). Former Prime Minister Yasuhiro Nakasone's official visit to this shrine in 1985 became a topic of international controversy, sparking a series of protests from China and domestic circles. A recent suggestion to remove the names of executed war criminals from the list of enshrined souls as a possible solution to the controversy was met with firm refusal by the shrine administration. Apparently the people in charge of the shrine were not eager to revoke the sanctity of deified souls. And because the government is unable to interfere with shrine affairs, since the Japanese Constitution guarantees the separation of state and religion, the war criminals remain deified.

Yasukuni Shrine's vast precincts cover some 1,076,400 square feet (100,000 square meters). The enormous steel *torii* gate which stands at the entrance to the approach to the shrine is the largest in Japan. Halfway down the approach is a bronze statue of Omura Masajiro, a hero of the Meiji Restoration and the first War Minister of the Meiji era. Further on stands another huge *torii*, this one of bronze, and just beyond is the magnificent main gate, its doors adorned with the Imperial crest of the sixteen-petaled chrysanthemum. The inner sanctuary is of the *shinmei* style of the ancient Ise shrines. In another hall are documents

The Budokan hall and Kitanomaru Koen Park

recording the official rank, surname, and personal history of each individual enshrined here.

A tour through the Yasukuni Shrine Museum (3261-8326; open 9:00 A.M.–5:00 P.M., until 4:30 P.M. November–March; closed December 28–31), located on the right side of the shrine's courtyard, is at once a grim and thought-provoking experience. Displayed in front of this military museum are weapons, including a naval gun and a tank. Exhibited inside are other war memorabilia, such as photos, letters, and uniforms of war heroes from the Meiji Restoration until World War II. At the center of the main hall is a Mitsubishi Zero fighter plane, around which are various machine guns and a model of the famous Japanese battleship *Yamato*. On the second floor are samurai armor, saddles, and early weapons.

The grounds at Yasukuni Shrine are shrouded with cherry blossoms in early April, and each spring a sumo tournament is held there.

Tourist Information

Travel Information
•**Tourist Information Center** (twenty-four hour recorded message)
English: 3503-2911

•**Japan National Tourist Organization, Tourist Information Center**
Kotani Building
1-6-6 Yurakucho
Chiyoda-ku, Tokyo
Telephone: 3502-1461-3
Toll-free outside Tokyo: 0120-222-800
(Open weekdays 9:00 A.M.–5:00 P.M., Saturdays 9:00 A.M.–Noon; closed Sundays and holidays.)

•**Asakusa Tourist Information Center**
(directly across the street from Kaminarimon gate)
Telephone: 3842-5566
(Open daily 9:30 A.M–8:00 P.M.)

Travel Agencies
•**American Express Travel Service**
American Express Tower
4-30-16, Ogikubo, Suginami-ku, Tokyo
Telephone: 3220-6320
Toll-free outside Tokyo: 0120-01-0120
(Open weekdays 9:00 A.M.–5:30 P.M., Fridays until 5:00 P.M..)

•**Japan Travel Bureau**
Nittetsu Nihonbashi Building
1-13-1 Nihonbashi, Tokyo
Chuo-ku, Tokyo
Telephone: 5620-9411
(Open daily 9:20 A.M.–6:00 P.M.)
English tourist information for package tours: 5620-9500

Branches are all over the city and most conveniently found in major city hotels. (Open 9:30 A.M.–5:30 P.M., Saturdays until 12:30 P.M., closed Sundays and holidays.)

Tokyo's Shitamachi

No tour of Tokyo can be complete without including the *shitamachi*, or "low city" (as opposed to the "high city" of the Yamanote area) at the east end of the capital. Steeped in the customs and culture of Edo's townspeople, *shitamachi* is still the home of the *edokko*, or "child of Edo," whose ancestors have lived and worked here for generations.

Ueno

One of the centers of the *shitamachi*, Ueno contains some of the most representative sightseeing spots in Tokyo. Originally a temple town, Ueno developed in the Edo era around the former Kaneiji temple, whose extensive precincts contained what is today **Ueno Park**. With the opening of Ueno Station in 1883, Ueno served as the gateway to the prosperous capital from northern Japan, and today is one of the busiest junctions in Tokyo.

Ueno Park

Located near Ueno Station, Japan's oldest public park (opened 1873) covers approximately 673,815 square feet (62,600 square meters). Its vast array of trees include numerous cherries, whose blossoms attract throngs of revelers during the flower-viewing season in early April. Its museums, temples, shrines, concert halls, zoo, historical monuments, gardens, and art university make Ueno Park one of the cultural gems of the capital.

At the southern entrance to the park, on a small plateau called Sakuragaoka ("Cherry Blossom Hill") stands one of the symbols of Ueno Park, the famous bronze statue of Saigo Takamori (completed 1898). Considered by many the quintessential hero of modern Japanese

Ueno Park's famed cherry blossoms

history, Saigo was the commander of the Imperial forces which defeated the armies of the Tokugawa Shogun. Just behind Saigo's statue is a shrine to a corps of his enemies—some 2,000 Tokugawa loyalists who fell near this site after being routed in a battle that led to the Meiji Restoration. There is an interesting woodblock print on display here, illustrating the scene of the bloody battle of Ueno Hill, as well as a small museum (open 10:00 A.M.–5:00 P.M., closed Thursdays).

Straight ahead on the left is **Kiyomizu Kannon-do** temple, which was built in 1631 in association with the famous Kiyomizu Temple in Kyoto. From the platform of this temple, in front of the altar, is a beautiful view of the wooded area below, and beyond this Shinobazu Pond.

Nearby is the **National Western Art Museum** (3828-5131; open, 9:30 A.M.–5:00 P.M.; closed Mondays [or Tuesdays when Mondays are holidays] and New Year's holidays; admission: ¥400), which features six bronze Rodins in its courtyard. Housed here are some 80 sculptures and 460 paintings, including the "Matsukata Collection," consisting of works from such masters as Cezanne, Monet, Manet, and Degas.

Towards the northern extremity of the park is the **Tokyo National Museum** (3822-1111; open 9:00 A.M.–4:30 P.M.; closed Mondays [or Tuesdays when Mondays are holidays] and New Year's holidays; admission: ¥400). Japan's largest museum, it consists of four separate buildings. The main building (opened 1938), with its Japanese-style tile roof over a European stone base, is in itself a work of art. Some 86,000 exhibits cover a wide range of oriental art, crafts, and ancient artifacts, including paintings, sculptures, swords, armor, metalwork, lacquer ware, ceramics, and textiles, 80 pieces of which are designated by the government as national treasures. To the immediate left of the main building (when approaching from the front gate) is the magnificent blue-domed **Hyokeikan** (completed 1909), whose archaeological collection consists of relics from prehistoric and ancient Japan. Designated an important cultural property, the building is representative of European-style architecture from the late Meiji era. Also contained within the spacious grounds of the

Tokyo National Museum in Ueno

National Museum is the **Black Gate**, another important cultural property. Erected as the front gate to the estate of a feudal lord in the late Edo period, it originally stood near Edo Castle.

Located between the National Western Art Museum and the Tokyo National Museum is the **National Science Museum** (3822-0111; open 9:00 A.M.–4:30 P.M.; closed Mondays [or Tuesdays when Mondays are holidays] and New Year's holidays; admission: ¥400). Divided into the departments of physics and chemistry, physical geography, zoology and botany, astronomy, meteorology, and oceanography, the entire museum is too big to take in during one visit.

West of here, on the other side of the open square below the fountain, are the **Ueno Zoological Gardens** (3828-5171; Open 9:30 A.M.–4:30 P.M.; closed Mondays or Tuesdays when Mondays are holidays]; admission: ¥400). Japan's oldest zoological park (opened 1882) is home to some 10,600 animals of about 800 species, the most popular of which is a family of four Chinese pandas. In the zoo's grounds stands the **Five-Storied Pagoda** of the former Keneiji temple.

In front of the National Western Art Museum

Built in 1631 by a leading Tokugawa vassal, this pagoda, whose reflection in the Shinobazu Pond is truly beautiful to behold, is another one of the park's important cultural properties.

The view of this pagoda is also exquisite from the grounds of the neighboring **Toshogu Shrine**, built in 1651 to enshrine Tokugawa Ieyasu. As magnificent as it is, this ornamental shrine compares neither in scale nor artistic achievement to the main Toshogu Shrine in Nikko. Stone lanterns which line the long entranceway were gifts to the Tokugawa Shogunate by feudal lords.

Concealed in the bushes next to the Seiyoken (one of Japan's first Western-style restaurants, opened 1876), is the **Toki-no-Kane** (constructed 1634), literally "Bell of Time." This belfry was one of nine in Edo which rang out the hours of day to the townspeople.

In the southwest portion of Ueno Park is the natural **Shinobazu Pond**, famous for its migratory birds and summer lotus flowers. Near the center of this pond, the northernmost one-third of which belongs to the zoo, is an island containing a shrine to Benten, the Goddess of Fortune. The path leading to the shrine is canopied with cherry blossoms during the spring. In the summer months the southern bank of the pond is the site of traditional festivities of old Edo. Also on the southern bank is **Tokyo Shitamachi Museum** (3823-7451; open 9:30 A.M.–4:30 P.M.; closed Mondays [or Tuesdays when Mondays are holidays]; admission: ¥200). This interesting little folk museum exhibits artifacts and utensils used by the commoners in Edo.

Ameya Yokocho

Descending from the lofty heights of **Ueno Park**—both geographically and cul-

Ameyoko is a scene of frenzied year-end shopping

turally speaking—you might have worked up an appetite for the plebeian side of Ueno. Spread out along the JR railroad tracks between Ueno and Okachimachi Stations is the open marketplace of **Ameya Yokocho**, more commonly known as "Ameyoko." Born out of the ruins of World War II, Ameyoko was originally a black market. According to one account, many of the items smuggled into this area came from the troops of the American Occupational Forces; thus the "Ame" (pronounced "Ah-may") of Ameyoko, or "America Alley." Today Ameyoko contains some 500 small shops and stalls, many of whose proprietors maintain the image, if not lineage, of the *shitamachi's edokko*. A trademark of this bustling marketplace is the constant shouting of merchants hawking their goods, which include wide varieties of dried and fresh fish and other edibles, clothing, camping equipment, and miscellaneous items, usually at bargain prices. Tucked into the maze of adjacent backstreets are various inexpensive eateries, including "stand-up" noodle counters. Even if you don't intend to buy anything, simply browsing through Ameyoko is an adventure in itself.

Asakusa

The *shitamachi* continues in nearby Asakusa, the site of the famed pleasure quarters of old Edo. Situated on the banks of the celebrated Sumida River, Edo's greatest waterway, Asakusa prospered as the town grew around the magnificent **Sensoji**, the oldest temple in the capital. After the Meiji Restoration, Asakusa became a gathering place for artists and intellectuals, who frequented the area's many opera houses, cinemas, and cafes. Though most of these establishments have long disappeared, Asakusa is one of the few areas in Tokyo which retains some of the earthy charm of old Edo.

Sensoji Temple and Surroundings

At the entrance of the shopping promenade called Nakamise, which is the approach to Sensoji temple, stands a gate whose tremendous power is reflected in its name **Kaminarimon**, or "Gate of Thunder." Hanging from the top of this gate is a giant vermillion-lacquered lantern. On its left, as you enter from the street, stands the ferocious God of Thunder, on the right the equally unnerving God of Wind. Behind the gate are two statues of dragon gods. Kaminarimon was reconstructed in 1960, ninety-five years after the former gate was destroyed by fire.

Sensoji Temple (3842-0181; open daily), founded in the seventh century, is dedicated to the Bodhisattva Kannon, or Goddess of Mercy, which may be compared to the Virgin Mary of Catholicism. According to legend, the Hinokuma brothers, Hamanari and Takenari, found a tiny golden statue of the goddess while fishing in the Sumida on 18 March 628. When they returned to their native village with their find, the village headman, Haji-no-Nakatomo, recognized the sancti-

ty of the Kannon, and enshrined it for all villagers to worship. Today this temple is one of the most famous centers of Kannon worship in Japan.

On the opposite end of the Nakamise shopping promenade is **Hozomon** gate, a ferroconcrete construction of the one lost in the World War II air raids. Standing guard on both sides of this gate are fierce Deva Kings, sculpted from cypress. Inside the gate are stored the valuable scriptures of Sensoji temple. These scriptures, printed in China in the fourteenth century, are designated national treasures. On the other side of this gate stands the magnificent main hall of Sensoji. Completed in 1958, it is a replica of the seventeenth-century structure built by the third Tokugawa Shogun Iemitsu, but lost in an air raid in 1945. Though the present building is made of ferroconcrete, it is true to the design of the old structure. The smoke from the incense burner at the center of the square in front of the main hall is said to be good for whatever ails you. For this you can thank the Goddess of Mercy, whose statue, having been buried deep in the ground during the war, survived the air raids. Today, the sacred statue is said to be locked inside the gold-plated inner shrine beyond the altar, and never revealed.

The five-storied pagoda to the left of the main hall, which is said to contain relics of the Buddha's bones, is also a concrete reconstruction of the Edo-era wooden original.

Just behind and to the right of the main hall is **Asakusa Shrine.** Dedicated to the two Hinokuma brothers (the finders of the Kannon statue) and their master Haji-no-Nakatomo, it is also called *Sanja-sama*, meaning shrine of the three (guardians). Constructed by Shogun

Kaminarimon: Sensoji Temple's Gate of Thunder

Iemitsu in the seventeenth century, the main structure remains unchanged, despite a major overhaul in 1960. The fabulous Sanja Festival, one of Tokyo's three biggest, is held here on Saturday and Sunday in mid-May. During this time the streets of Asakusa are filled with joy and laughter, and some one hundred mikoshi (portable shrines) are carried by thousands of traditionally-clad revelers. At the beginning of October is the Edo Mikoshi Festival, a parade of some twenty portable shrines which are carried through the surrounding streets, starting and ending at Asakusa Shrine. (For information on the schedules of these festivals and other events and attractions, visit the Asakusa Tourist Information Center, which is across the street from Kaminarimon gate.)

The east entrance to Sensoji temple is **Nitenmon** gate. Built in 1681 for use by the Tokugawa Shogun, this original gate survived the air raids of World War II.

On the right side of the Nakamise shopping promenade, before you get to Hozomon gate, is **Bentenyama** ("Benten Hill"), the site of an ancient burial mound. There is a shrine here dedicated to Benten, the Goddess of Fortune. Next to this is the famous **Bentenyama Belfry**. The bell retains its original shape, and still rings once a day at 6:00 A.M., and on New Year's Eve.

Denbo-in, located to the left of Nakamise before you reach Hozomon gate, is a subordinate facility of Sensoji temple. Built in 1777, it consists of a guest hall, the chief abbot's living quarters and other sections. Its gorgeous garden, designed in the first half of the seventeenth century, contains a large pond at its center, the surrounding path of which is similar to that of the one at the famous Katsura Detached Palace in Kyoto. In the corner of the garden is the replica of a famous eighteenth-century Kyoto tea house which is now lost. The garden is not open to the public, but viewing is allowed by appointment (call or visit Sensoji main office, to the left of the pagoda near the main hall).

There are a number of quaint little restaurants and drinking establishments on the side streets behind Denbo-in. Walk around here in the early evening for a glimpse of the atmosphere of old-fashioned Tokyo. Most of these places are open in the afternoon, and closing time is generally early, around 9:00 or 10:00 P.M.

Just to the left of Sensoji temple's main hall is Asakusa Okuyama-en (3844-5656; open daily, 9:00 A.M.–7:00 P.M.), which houses the **Asakusa Nigiwai Museum** (admission: ¥350). Through the life-size models, pictures, and an interesting sort of mechanical puppet show, this museum gives a picture of the town of Asakusa, including Sensoji temple, the Nakamise shopping promenade, the Yoshiwara pleasure quarter, and the opera houses and cafes from the Edo period until the days just after World War II.

Sumida River

So important was the Sumida to the people of old Edo that they often referred to it as "big river." Edo's culture developed along its banks, where cherries blossomed in the spring, and fireworks lit the sky. Sumo tournaments were held along the Sumida, as were the great festivals of Asakusa and Fukagawa. The "big river" attracted poets, writers, and other artists, including Katsushika Hokusai (1760–1849), celebrated for his woodblock prints but who also painted illustrious scenes of everyday life along the Sumida. Icefish and carp were plentiful in this river, where the edible Asakusa *nori* was cultivated. The Sumida was once so pure that it was used for brewing sake. But with the industrialization which began in the early twentieth century the Sumida became so polluted that it was nicknamed "River of Death." In recent years, however, the river has shown signs of revitalization.

Hokusai included in his paintings a number of the beautiful arched wooden bridges which spanned the Sumida during the Edo period. Today, of course, these have been replaced with twenty-eight modern structures.

Across the busy street from Azumabashi Bridge, on the main intersection near Asakusa Station, is the famous **Kamiya Bar** (3841-5400; open 11:30 A.M.–10:00 P.M.; closed Tuesdays). Established in 1880, Japan's first Western-style bar is famous for its house cocktail, Denki-Bran ("Electric Brandy"), a potent concoction mixing vermouth, curaçao, gin, and wine to a brandy base. The restaurant on the second floor offers good Japanese Western-style cuisine at reasonable prices.

The Sumida River sightseeing boat (3841-9178) leaves from the left side of Azumabashi Bridge, near Sumida Park, every forty minutes on weekdays between 9:50 A.M. to 6:15 P.M. The fare depends on your point of destination, of which there are two. It costs ¥560 to get to the Takeshiba Pier terminal, where you will have a good view of the ocean and the ships in Tokyo Harbor. The fare to the other destination, **Hamarikyu Garden** (3541-0200; open 9:00 A.M.–4:30 P.M.; closed Mondays —if Monday is a holiday, it will be closed on Tuesday—and New Year's holidays), is ¥720, which includes the ¥200 entrance fee to the garden. This garden was originally the hawking grounds of the shoguns, and later became a part of the Imperial Detached Palace. Situated on Tokyo Bay and flanked by the Tsukiji and Shiodome rivers, the garden's expansive landscape is typical of those of feudal lords of the Edo period. (You can catch return boats to Asakusa from either destination.)

Just above Hamarikyu Garden, where the Sumida meets the smaller Tsukiji River, is **Tsukiji Wholesale Fishmarket**. A short walk from Tsukiji Station on the Hibiya Subway Line, this is one of the world's largest fish markets, where 90 percent of Tokyo's fish is sold. Frozen fish from all over the world and fresh fare caught off Japan are auctioned here to wholesalers each morning. The quality is supreme, the fish the freshest. The best tuna, many of which are caught in the South Pacific, cost thousands of dollars each. Bidding starts at 5:00 A.M., but the busiest hours—and best time to visit—are between 6:00 A.M. and 8:00 A.M. After the auctioning, the wholesalers display their seafood in their own stalls in the market for sale to professional chefs and restaurant owners who come from all over Tokyo and the surrounding area. After taking in all of the hustle and bustle of the early morning Tsukiji Wholesale Fishmarket, breakfast at

A shop specializing in traditional foods

one of the nearby restaurants is an experience not to be missed.

Well south of Asakusa and across the
Sumida River is **Fukagawa**, a flourishing
center of old Edo. The wealthy merchants of Fukagawa patronized a bur-
geoning culture, which attracted people
of all classes to this town to spend their
leisure hours. Here were great sumo
tournaments, festivals, boating on the
Sumida, and geisha houses.

For a trip back in time to the Fukagawa
of the Edo period visit the **Fukagawa Edo
Museum** (3630-0025; open daily 10:00
A.M.–5:00 P.M.; closed New Year's holidays; admission: ¥300) located fifteen-
minute walk from Monzen-Nakacho
(Tozai Subway Line) or Morishita (Toei
Shinjuku Subway Line) Stations, which
has reproduced a life-sized section of the
town as it appeared in the mid-nineteenth
century. The museum presents replicas of
the past while reviving the spiritual heritage of this once bustling town along the
Sumida, all with a great deal of precision
and authenticity. Weave your way
through the crowded ante-room, where
you will encounter a sumo wrestler, a tea

stall waitress, a carpenter, a traveling
musician, a fortune teller, and others, all
cleverly painted on glass for a realistic
effect. Next, descend the stairway and
enter another world, reproduced in exact
detail from new materials which have
been made to look old. The lighting and
sound effects of the mock town are
changed to represent different times of
day. A rooster's crowing and the calls of
street hawkers are heard in "the morning." At "six o-clock in the evening" a
temple bell rings, and an "orange sunset"
paints the wall by the canal in front of the
boathouse-tavern. The location of the
buildings and layout of the town is based
on an old map of a section of Fukagawa
called Saga-cho, on the east side of the
Sumida. Pass by the wholesaler's shop
and warehouse, until you come to the
vegetable store. After browsing here and
at the rice shop next-door, step into the
boathouse tavern and make yourself at
home. (Don't forget to remove your shoes
before entering.) The proprietor Gonzo is
thirty-five years old, his wife Okei thirty.
Go outside and have a look at the small
boat moored in the canal. Take a rest at
the tea stall, noticing the traditional layout of the benches, tea utensils and water
cask. On the street behind this visit the
tenement home of the forty-year-old
sawyer Daikichi, and his thirty-five-year-
old wife Otaka. Feel free to enter and sit
on the wooden floor among exact replicas
of the furniture that these two natives of
Fukagawa actually used. In the next
house lives the boatman Matsujiro, who is
twenty-three and still single. Take a good
look and you'll notice that Matsujiro's
home is a bit messier than that of the
widow next-door, Oshizu. All of these
tenants share the same well, which is situated at the center of the the small complex, near the common outhouse.

Tokyo Disneyland

Tokyo Disneyland (0473-54-0001), owned and operated entirely by Oriental Land Co., Ltd., held its grand opening in April 1983. With the Walt Disney Company contributing the master planning, operational expertise, use of the Disneyland name, and copyrighted materials, the Tokyo Disneyland theme park is basically a replica of its American counterparts, only larger. In fact, the Tokyo theme park, which attracts over sixteen million people annually, covers an area of 46.2 hectares (114.2 acres) (the Disneyland theme park in Anaheim is 30 hectares, the one in Florida 43 hectares). Five theme lands (World Bazaar, Adventureland, Westernland, Fantasyland, Tomorrowland) encompass thirty-six attractions, thirty-two restaurants, and fifty shops. The park stage seventeen live entertainment shows, boasting the largest working costume wardrobe in the Far East.

Tokyo Disneyland, officially part of **Tokyo Bay Resort City Maihama**, which includes five deluxe hotels built along the waterfront, is walking distance from Maihama Station (seventeen minutes from Tokyo Station by the JR Keiyo Line).

The park's operating hours vary depending on the day of the month. A Tokyo Disneyland Passport, an all-inclusive ticket good for general admission and almost all attractions, costs ¥4,400 for adults, ¥4,000 for juniors (ages twelve through seventeen), and ¥3,000 for children (ages four through eleven). Inquire about tickets and bus transportation at the Disneyland ticket center at Tokyo Station (north Yaesu exit).

Tokyo Bay Resort City Maihama

The Tokyo Stock Exchange

The **Tokyo Stock Exchange** (3666-0141) is located in the district of Kabuto-cho, a name which has become synonymous with TSE itself. Kabuto-cho is near Kayaba-cho Station (Tozai and Hibiya Subway Lines) and Nihombashi Station (Toei Asakusa Subway Line). Open Monday through Friday (except national holidays, December 31, and the first three days of each year), the Exchange welcomes all visitors, but groups are asked to give advance notice of intended visits. Trading hours are from 9:00 A.M. to 11:00 A.M., and 1:00 P.M. to 3:00 P.M. A complete guide to TSE, including explanations of trading rules and procedures and the layout of the stock trading floor, is provided in English. Admission is free to the TSE Exhibition Plaza (open 9:00 A.M.–4:00 P.M.), where visitors can watch the stock trading floor activities from the gallery on the second floor. Plaza exhibits explain the history and current roles of TSE, as well as stock exchanges and investment information around the world. Guided tours to the TSE Exhibition Plaza are available in English.

Established in 1878 as Tokyo Stock Exchange Co., Ltd., the TSE was founded in its present form in April 1949. The trading of stocks started shortly thereafter, with bonds first being traded here in April 1956. Government bonds were listed for the first time after World War II in October 1966, and the TSE stock price index (TOPIX) inaugurated in July 1969. The Exchange's Foreign Stock Section was opened in December 1973, bringing on its heels the implementation of the Computerized Market Information System in September 1974. In February of 1986 ten security companies, including TSE's first six foreign firms, joined the Exchange, with the number of foreign companies increasing to sixteen in May of 1988. Trading in stock index futures based on TOPIX was initiated in the fall of 1988, and trading on stock index (TOPIX) options began in October 1989. By the end of the same year trading in U.S. Treasury Bond (T-Bond) futures had begun, followed by options on Japanese government bond futures trading in May 1990. TSE utilizes state-of-the-art electronic and communications technology for trading in order to provide the fairest and most efficient market place possible.

The Tokyo Stock Exchange, the world's second largest

Forums for Sports, Music, and Business

Tokyo Dome

Tokyo Dome (near Suidobashi Station, on the JR Sobu and Mita Subway Lines), the home of the Tokyo Giants and Nippon Ham Fighters, is more than just Japan's only indoor baseball stadium. Also called the Big Egg, this high-tech forum with a seating capacity of 56,000 is the venue of other major events, including American football games, soccer matches, rock concerts, trade exhibitions, and business conventions. Completed in 1988, its magnificent white dome is sustained by an air-support system, by which the air pressure inside is three percent higher than the air pressure outside. Made of specially-developed, lightweight teflon-coated glass, the dome allows in enough sunlight during the daytime to make lighting unnecessary. The field can be widened by means of the world's first movable seats in both right and left fields.

Nippon Convention Center

The **Nippon Convention Center** (NCC), also called *Makuhari Messe* (043-296-0001), backs up its claim to be "an international meeting stage for people, goods, information and services" by boasting the largest exhibition and convention facility in Japan. Featuring a wide spectrum of state-of-the-art technology, NCC's main assets consist of three facilities—International Exhibition Hall, International Conference Hall, and Makuhari Event Hall—which cover an astounding 1,829,880 square feet (170,000 square meters). The three halls have been designed for a variety of events, including trade shows, concerts, exhibitions, fashion shows, and sporting events.

NCC is situated at the center of Chiba Prefecture's **Makuhari New Town**, forty minutes from Tokyo Station on the JR Keiyo Line. (Get off at Kaihin Makuhari Station, just a five-minute walk from the convention center.) Conveniently built halfway between the center of Tokyo and Narita Airport on reclaimed land in Tokyo Bay, Makuhari New Town is being promoted by the Chiba Prefectural government as an international information city for the twenty-first century.

Tokyo International Trade Center

The **Tokyo International Trade Center** at Harumi comprises the largest trade fair and exhibition grounds in Tokyo, and the second largest in Japan after NCC. Founded in April 1958, the trade center was moved to reclaimed land on Tokyo Bay in the following year. Consisting of seven exhibition halls with a combined exhibition area of 604,212 square feet (56,162 square meters), the trade center holds approximately 100 events each year, which attract some five million visitors.

Tokyo International Trade Center publishes its semiannual *Trade Center News* (January and July) in both Japanese and English, which lists and briefly describes the events scheduled during the ensuing six-month period. Recent major events have included the Tokyo Auto Salon, Marine Festival, and the International Gift Show.

Makuhari Messe *is a major convention center*

Places of Interest

Tokyo has much to offer in the way of museums, galleries, parks and gardens, and amusement parks. Since traveling between sights can take up valuable time, refer to the specific area guides for help in planning your day's itinerary. The **Tokyo National Museum** is probably a must-see, simply because it has one of the world's finest collections of Asian art, but don't overlook the smaller collections of former nobility or Japanese business magnates, or the excellent art shows staged by department stores such as Takashimaya, Seibu, and Isetan. Most museums and many parks are closed on Mondays, or the following day if Monday happens to be a national holiday. (Check entries or call in advance.) For current attractions, a good source is *The Japan Times* Saturday edition, and *Tokyo Journal*, a monthly English magazine also listing film, theater, and dance performances.

Art Museums

Bridgestone Museum of Art (3563-0241)
Goto Art Museum (3703-0661)
Hara Museum of Contemporary Art (3445-0651)
Hatakeyama Museum (3447-5787)
Idemitsu Art Museum (3213-9402)
Kuroda Memorial Hall, Tokyo National Research Institute of Cultural Properties (3823-2241)
Museum of Tokyo National University of Fine Arts and Music (3828-6111)
National Museum of Modern Art (3214-2561)
National Museum of Western Art (3828-5131)
Nezu Art Museum (3400-2536)
Okura Shukokan Museum (3583-0781)
Ota Museum of Art (3403-0880)
Riccar Art Museum (3571-3254)
Setagaya Art Museum (3415-6011)
Sezon Museum of Art (5992-0155)
Sogetsu Art Museum/Sogetsu Art Gallery (3408-1126)
Suntory Museum of Art (3470-1073)
Tokyo Metropolitan Art Museum (3823-6921)
Tokyo Metropolitan Museum of Photography (3280-0031)
Tokyo Metropolitan Teien Art Museum (3443-3227)
Tokyo National Museum (3822-1111)
Ueno no Mori Art Museum (3833-4191)

History and Culture Museums

Ancient Orient Museum (3989-3491)
Crafts Gallery of the National Museum of Modern Art (3211-7781)
Daimyo Clock Museum (3821-6913)
Fukugawa Edo Museum (3630-8625)
Furniture Museum (3533-0098)
Japan Folk Crafts Museum (3467-4527)
Japanese Sword Museum (3379-1386)
Meiji University Museums (3296-4431)
Paper Museum (3911-3545)
Shitamachi Museum (3823-7451)
Sumo Museum (3622-0366)
Tobacco and Salt Museum (3476-2041)
Tokyo Metropolitan Modern Literature Museum (3466-5150)
Transportation Museum (3251-8481)
Waseda University Theater Museum (3203-4141)
Yasukuni Shrine Museum (3261-8326)

Science and Technology Museums

Nac Image Engineering Exhibition Hall (3403-7176)
National Science Museum (3822-0111)
NHK Broadcasting Museum (5400-6900)
Science and Technology Museum (3212-8471)
Ship Museum (3528-1111)

Galleries / Special-Interest Exhibit Spaces

INAX Gallery (5250-6530)
Japan Calligraphy Museum (3965-2611)
Kamakura Gallery (3574-8307)
Kite Museum (3275-2704)
Kobayashi Gallery (3561-0515)
Nihon Saké Center (3575-0656)
Nishimura Gallery (3567-3906)
Photo Gallery International (3501-9123)
P3 Alternative Museum Tokyo (3353-6866)
Sanrio Gallery (3563-2731)
Satani Gallery (3564-6733)
Spiral Garden (3498-1171)
Tokyo Designers Space (3587-2007)
Watari-Um Museum of Contemporary Art (3402-3001)
Zeit Photo Salon (3246-1370)

Botanical / Zoological Gardens and Parks

Baji Park
Denboin Garden
Hama Detached Palace Garden
Hibiya Park
Imperial Palace East Garden
Kinuta Ryokuchi Park
Kiyosumi Garden
Koishikawa Botanical Gardens
Meiji Shrine
Mukojima Botanical Gardens
Rikugien Garden
Shinjuku Gyoen
Shinobazu Pond and Bentendo
Tama Zoological Park
Tokyo Metropolitan Wild Bird Park
Ueno Zoological Gardens
Yoyogi Park
Yumenoshima Tropical Plant Dome

Aquariums and Amusement Parks

Hanayashiki Amusement Park (3842-8780)
Korakuen Amusement Park (5800-9999)
Sanrio Puroland (0423-39-1111)
Seibuen Amusement Park (0429-22-1371)
Sunshine International Aquarium (3989-3466)
Tokyo Disneyland (0473-54-0001)
Tokyo Sea Life Park (3869-5151)
Toshimaen Amusement Park (3990-3131)
Ueno Zoo Aquarium (3828-5171)
Yomiuri Land (044-966-1111)

Suggested Destinations Outside Tokyo

Although the Japanese capital is indeed the economic, political, and in many ways cultural center of modern Japan, there are a great number of places around the nation which deserve mention. Since it would be impossible to discuss more than just a few of these here, we have selected Japan's largest cities and business centers outside of Tokyo (Yokohama, Osaka, Nagoya, Sapporo, Kyoto, Fukuoka), five of which (Sapporo is the exception) are connected to the capital by the Shinkansen bullet train, and all of which are within easy access to airports served regularly by All Nippon Airways and other domestic airlines. We have also included the towns of Nara, Nikko, and Kamakura, which, along with Kyoto, contain some of Japan's greatest cultural treasures. Finally, the hot springs mountain resort of Hakone is on our list of suggested destinations for its proximity to Tokyo and fabulous views of Mt. Fuji.

Nikko

N|ikko National Park, a historic retreat in the deeply forested mountains eighty miles (128 kilometers) north of Tokyo, is a short two hours by limited express on the Tobu Line from Tobu-Asakusa Station. Besides its many cultural treasures, Nikko's attractions include the scenic **Lake Chuzenji**, the spectacular **Kegon no Taki** falls, and an abundance of hot spring baths.

Nikko's history stretches back to the eighth century, when a monastery for Buddhist asceticism was established here. Nikko remained a center of Buddhism until it was suppressed by the great warlord Toyotomi Hideyoshi at the end of the sixteenth century. Today, Nikko is most famous as the site of the magnificent **Toshogu Shrine**, which enshrines Tokugawa Ieyasu, the illustrious founder of the Tokugawa Shogunate, and perhaps the most important figure in Japanese history. The Nikko Toshogu was completed and dedicated to Ieyasu a year after his death in 1616. His remains are buried here. (Also honored at Toshogu are Hideyoshi and the first shogun, Minamoto Yoritomo.)

Nikko Sights

Before reaching the main approach to Toshogu, you will come to the Tendai temple of **Rinno-ji**. Founded some 1,200 years ago, Rinno-ji served as the center of religious activity in Nikko until the seventeenth century. Inside the temple's Hall of the Three Buddhas are three giant gilt statues, said to be the largest Buddhist sculptures of their kind in Japan.

Beyond the temple is the main approach to **Toshogu Shrine**. Toshogu's unsurpassed ornateness—emphasized by the famous expression "Never say *kekko* (good) until you've seen Nikko!"—is due greatly to the efforts of Ieyasu's grandson, Iemitsu, who rebuilt the shrine in 1636. It is estimated that Iemitsu, the third Tokugawa Shogun, spent the equivalent of $200 million in today's currency constructing this shrine.

The granite *torii* gate (built 1618) on the main approach to the shrine is one of the largest of its kind in Japan. Beyond the vermillion **Omotemon** gate, the only entrance to the shrine, are three warehouses which contain sacred ritual objects. (Among these are costumes and equipment used twice a year, on May 18 and October 17, for the Festival of the Procession of the Warriors.) On the left is the sacred stable, carved with the **Three Wise Monkeys**, "Hear no Evil, Speak no Evil, See no Evil."

You will also see the brilliantly decorated **Yomeimon** gate, a national treasure with over 400 carvings. Painted in shades of gold, vermillion, green, and blue, these carvings include lions, tigers, dragons and various mythical creatures, Chinese sages, and children. (Lower-ranked samurai were not permitted past

Picturesque Toshogu Shrine in Nikko

this gate, while those of the higher ranks were obliged to remove their swords before entering.) Just to the left of Yomeimon is **Honji-do** hall (a reconstruction of the original destroyed by fire in 1961), famous for the drawing of the so-called crying dragon on its ceiling. If you stand directly beneath the dragon and clap your hands, the resulting echo sounds like the mythical beast crying.

Yomeimon is flanked by ornate fences and corridors, also national treasures, which enclose the inner compound. On the left side is **Jinyo-sha**, which stores the three portable shrines for the three souls (Ieyasu, Hideyoshi, Yoritomo) honored at Toshogu. The unusually designed **Chinese Gate**, another national treasure, is the innermost portal of the shrine. Curled up in the East Corridor toward Sakashitamon is yet another national treasure, the famous **Sleeping Cat** carving.

The innermost buildings of Toshogu are the Haiden oratory and the Main Hall. The east antechamber of the Haiden was reserved for the Shogun and the three Tokugawa-branch houses of Owari, Kii, and Mito. The tomb of Tokugawa Ieyasu is located at the top of the long flight of steps beyond Sakashitamon.

Just west of Toshogu is **Futara-san Jinja** shrine, the Shinto center of Nikko for the eight centuries before the establishment of Toshogu. Futara-san Jinja's bronze *torii* gate and colorful halls are designated important cultural properties. Perhaps the most famous attraction here is an antique bronze Goblin Lantern. According to legend, this lantern assumed supernatural shapes after nightfall. One night a terrified samurai attacked it with his sword, and the marks left are still visible on its rim.

A short southwesterly walk from Futara-san Jinja will bring you to **Taiyuin**

Yomeimon Gate, the most ornate of National Treasures

Mausoleum. Set in a dense cedar forest, this mausoleum of the Shogun Tokugawa Iemitsu was completed in 1653. Iemitsu was responsible for securing Tokugawa authority over the feudal lords by, among other things, enforcing the system of alternate attendance at Edo, closing Japan to the outside world, and banning the building of large ships to ensure that the country would remain isolated. Having worshipped his grandfather Ieyasu, Iemitsu had his own mausoleum built in a similar style to Toshogu, but smaller in scale. As a result, Taiyuin is considered esthetically superior to the perhaps overly ornate Toshogu. There are sacred warehouses here, reminiscent of those at Toshogu, beautiful gilded and lacquered gates, and a Main Hall. The Haiden oratory is a national treasure which contains a beautiful panel portraying three Chinese lions on a background of gold leaf. To the right is Kokamon gate, a white plaster Chinese structure. Beyond the gate lies Iemitsu's cast-bronze tomb, but unfortunately entrance is prohibited.

Kamakura

Kamakura, the seat of Japan's first military government (see "Historical Introduction"), is located on the coast of Sagami Bay just an hour southwest of Tokyo (from Tokyo or Shinagawa Stations) on the Yokosuka Line. This scenic seaside retreat, surrounded on three sides by forested hills, is home to numerous ancient temples and shrines which reflect the ascetic values of the warriors and priests who dominated Japan during the Kamakura Period (1185-1333). Kamakura witnessed the origins of Zen and the shoguns, and it is in this peaceful setting that Japan's samurai class rose to prominence. The Buddhist cult of the savior Amida flourished in Kamakura, memorialized by the 121-ton bronze statue of the **Great Buddha** which is located there. Just north, at Kita Kamakura, are two of Japan's oldest Zen monasteries, **Kencho-ji** and **Engaku-ji**. At the center of Kamakura is **Tsurugaoka Hachiman-gu**, the tutelary shrine of Minamoto Yoritomo, Japan's first shogun and founder of the Kamakura Shogunate in 1192.

The Kencho-ji temple

Sights in Kamakura

For sightseeing purposes, Kamakura can be divided into three areas: Kita (or north) Kamakura, whose station by the same name is one stop before Kamakura Station on the Yokosuka Line; Central Kamakura, most readily accessible from Kamakura Station itself; and the vicinity of the Great Buddha, which is a fifteen-minute bus ride from Kamakura Station. As one visit does not allow enough time to see more than a few of the numerous cultural treasures this town has to offer, selections are offered from each of these areas.

Since Kamakura is the place where Zen took root in Japan, many of its temples are dedicated to this Buddhist sect, the most important of which are located in the tranquil, forested mountains of Kita Kamakura. The outer gate of **Engaku-ji temple** (open 8:00 A.M.–4:30 P.M., in summer until 5:30 P.M.) is situated by Kita Kamakura Station. Engaku-ji was built in 1282 by the regent Hojo Tokimune, to console the souls of warriors killed in the second Mongol invasion of 1281. Today this temple is well-known outside of Japan in connection with the famous Zen philosopher Daisetsu Suzuki (1870–1966), author of many books on Zen in English, who was a disciple of the Zen master Shaku Soen, a chief abbot of Engaku-ji.

After passing through the outer gate of Engaku-ji, you will reach the great two-storied **Sanmon** gate (the main gate) which marks the entrance to the temple proper. Unlike most of the buildings of this ancient temple, Sanmon escaped the ravages of the Great Kanto Earthquake of 1923. In the nearby garden stands a majestic **700-year-old juniper tree**, a designated natural monument.

The Great Bell (built 1301), located up

Buddhist monks at Kencho-ji

the slope to the right and accessible by a flight of stone steps, is a national treasure whose exquisite symmetry typifies Kamakura-era craftsmanship.

To the left of Sanmon gate is another national treasure, the **Relic Hall**, which is said to enshrine some of the sacred ashes of the Buddha. This arched-roof building is considered to be the finest example of Zen-style Sung architecture in Japan. Although the age of the Relic Hall is unknown, it is believed to have been moved to its present site from a Kamakura convent during the Muromachi period (1392–1573).

The nearby **Butsunichian** is a pleasant place to relax over a bowl of *matcha* (powdered green tea used in the tea ceremony). There is also a tea house here which the Nobel laureate Yasunari Kawabata used as the setting for his famous novel *Thousand Cranes*.

Across the narrow road from Engaku-ji is **Tokei-ji** (open 8:30 A.M. –5:00 P.M.), a Buddhist temple of a much different nature. Also known as Kakekomi-dera ("Run-in Temple") and Enkiri-dera

("Divorce Temple"), Tokei-ji was founded in 1285 by the nun Kakuzan (the widow of the regent Hojo Tokimune) as a sanctuary for abused wives seeking divorce from their husbands.

Among the exhibits in the temple's Treasure Hall are two important cultural properties: a rare lacquerware box for consecrated bread of the Catholic religion, with the emblem of the Jesuits on its lid, and an incense burner. In the early spring the plum trees near the small thatched-roof Sanmon gate to this temple are covered with blossoms. Later the grounds of Tokei-ji are adorned with beautiful cherries and magnolias, and in other seasons hydrangeas, irises, cosmos, and camellias are in bloom.

Nearby is **Jochi-ji**, founded in 1281 by Munemasa Hojo, the younger brother of the regent Hojo Tokimune. This temple is also noted for its beautiful flowers all year around. In the Buddha Hall are three wooden images of the Buddhas Amida, Shaka, and Miroku, representing the three phases of the temporal world: past, present, and future.

A ten-minute stroll down the main road, away from Kita Kamakura Station, will bring you to **Kencho-ji** (open 8.30 A.M.–4:30 P.M.), built in 1253 by the

Sentai Jizo statue at Hasedera temple

regent Hojo Tokiyori. The regent appointed the priest Rankei Doryu (1214–1278) from Sung-dynasty China as its first abbot. It was Rankei who actively introduced Zen Buddhism to Japan. A painting of this priest, which is a national treasure, is among the wealth of objects displayed here every year in the first three days of November.

To the right of the magnificent San-mon gate is a great bell, another national treasure, which was cast in 1255. The approach to the Buddha Hall is lined with junipers, believed to have been planted some seven centuries ago with seeds brought from China by Rankei Doryu. Kencho-ji is unique among Zen temples in that its Buddha Hall does not

Kamakura's Great Buddha

enshrine an image of the Buddha but a large seated statue of the bodhisattva Jizo.

Take the bus from Kencho-ji bus stop to Kamakura Station to get to Central Kamakura. From the east side of the station approach the wide Wakamiya-oji, the historical avenue leading to the greatest attraction in this part of the town, **Tsurugaoka Hachiman-gu** shrine. This avenue is arched by three great *torii* gates built in 1182 by the first shogun, Minamoto Yoritomo, to safeguard the health of his pregnant wife, Masako.

The raised main approach to the shrine is lined with cherry trees between the second and third *torii*, and in the spring becomes a gorgeous tunnel of blossoms. The original shrine was founded near Kamakura Bay in 1063 by an ancestor of Yoritomo, dedicated to the Japanese god of war, Hachiman, tutelary deity of the Minamoto clan. In 1180 Yoritomo moved the shrine to its present site, on a hill overlooking the headquarters of his military government.

The **Kamakura National Treasure Hall** within the shrine compound houses some 2,000 treasures belonging to Kamakura temples, mostly from the Kamakura and Muromachi eras (1192–1573). Available here is an English brochure describing the monthly changing exhibits. Special exibits consisting solely of national treasures and important cultural properties are put on several times a year.

The **Great Buddha,** one of the most famous sites in Japan, is a fifteen-minute bus ride from Kamakura Station. This magnificent statue of the Amida Buddha, built in 1253, is an extraordinary example of perfectly proportioned features despite its tremendous size. This national treasure is the second largest statue in Japan after the Great Buddha at Nara's Todai-ji temple.

Hakone

Hakone is a national park and mountain resort only one and a half hours from Tokyo (from Shinjuku Station by the Odakyu Line's "Romance Car" express). Hakone's proximity to the capital makes it ideal for the busy traveler who would like to squeeze in a night at an authentic hot spring spa, and the area has over a dozen to choose from. Situated in the crater of an ancient volcano, Hakone's views of Mt. Fuji have attracted vacationers since time immemorial.

The final station along the Odakyu Line is **Hakone-Yumoto**. Here is the largest of Hakone's hot spring spas, and possibly the most famous in Japan. If the town's souvenir shops and throngs of tourists are too much for you, take the short, scenic ride on the mountain tram (Hakone Tozan Tetsudo Line) from here to **Miyanoshita**, the oldest resort spa in the area. Here are some of Hakone's most famous hotels—including the Fujiya, Japan's second oldest existing Western hotel, and the Naraya Ryokan, which dates back to the Edo period. Miyanosita has several art and antique shops that are interesting to browse through. Cut into the rocks of a nearby river is the **Taiko no Iwaburo** bath, believed to have been used by the famous warlord Toyotomi Hideyoshi.

Further along the mountain tram (forty minutes from Yumoto) near the summit of Mt. Soun-zan, is the wooded resort spa of **Gora**. From Gora a funicular railway climbs to the summit, where you can catch a cable car ride (the second longest in the world) down Mt. Soun-zan to Togendai on the north shore of Lake Ashi. From Togendai you can board a sightseeing boat to Hakone-machi across the lake, where you will find an exact reproduction of the **Hakone Checkpoint**.

Mt. Fuji provides a beautiful backdrop for Lake Ashi

During the Edo period travelers along the Tokaido, the main highway connecting Edo and Kyoto, had to display permits to be allowed to pass the Hakone Checkpoint. Inside, lifesize wax models of samurai guards are displayed checking travel documents and searching travelers for smuggled weapons and other banned items. The nearby museum exhibits weapons, records of early foreign travelers, and photographs of people crucified or beheaded for attempting to sneak across the pass.

In the icy water along the lake's western shore, in Moto-Hakone, stands the red *torii* gate of **Hakone Shrine**. Founded in A.D. 757, the shrine is famous as the one-time abode of a twelfth-century samurai who avenged the murder of his father. There is an old battered tree trunk, part way up the steep stone stairway on the approach to the shrine, which the samurai is said to have struck with a training sword tens of thousands of times while in preparation to kill his father's murderer. The sword believed used for the actual act of vengeance is displayed in the nearby Treasure House.

Yokohama

Yokohama, Japan's largest port, second most populous city (over three million), and a major industrial area, is located thirty minutes from Tokyo Station on the Yokosuka Line (twenty-two minutes from Shinagawa Station). Yokohama was a remote fishing village until Japan was opened to the rest of the world in 1859 and the foreign district of **Kannai** was established here. Today the city's main commercial and shopping district is centered around Yokohama Station, the transportation and business hub of Kanagawa Prefecture.

Yokohama Sights

After the Meiji Restoration, Kannai (five minutes from Yokohama Station on the JR Negishi Line) flourished as a center of international trade, and today the district is one of the main tourist spots in Yokohama. Kannai still retains its old European flavor in some of its buildings and monuments, the street lanterns, sidewalks paved with red bricks, and red-brick buildings. Among Kannai's Meiji-era buildings is the bronze-domed **Kanagawa Prefectural Museum** (045-201-0926; open 9:00 A.M.–4:00 P.M.; closed Mondays), a neo-Baroque structure built in 1904 as a bank headquarters. Among the museum's exhibits is an interesting collection of woodblock prints portraying Yokohama of the mid-nineteenth century.

The red-brick **Yokohama-shi Kaikou Kinenkan Memorial Museum** (045-201-0708; closed Monday and the day after a holiday), an important cultural property, was completed in 1917 to commemorate the fiftieth anniversary of the opening of Yokohama Port. The building's picturesque clock tower and stained glass windows are particularly popular among tourists, who may enter freely.

Yokohama's Chinatown at night.

Just southwest of Kannai at Yokohama Port is a new waterfront district, scheduled for completion in the year 2000. Just a short walk from Sakuragi-cho Station on the Toyoko Line, the new waterfront will include Japan's tallest building (seventy-three stories) and the world's most advanced convention center. Already open to the public here is the **Yokohama Museum of Art** (045-211-0300; open 10:00 A.M.–6:00 P.M., closed Thursdays), whose collection includes paintings from such masters as Cezanne, Dali, and Ernst, and photographs by Edward Steichen and Kimura Ihei.

Also completed along the waterfront is **Nippon Maru Memorial Park**, which features the *Nippon Maru* sailing vessel. Nicknamed "White Bird," this beautiful ship, which sailed around the world forty-five times over a half a century, is permanently moored at Yokohama, and may be boarded and explored.

Not to be missed is Yokohama's **Chinatown**, located west of Kannai, a ten-minute walk from Ishikawa-cho Station on the JR Negishi Line. Chinatown was established by the Japanese government in 1899 as a residential and business district for the nation's Chinese population. Today its bustling streets are lined with a myriad of Chinese restaurants and interesting import shops.

Kyoto

Kyoto (population about 1,500,000), Japan's former capital for over a millennium and the home of the emperor from A.D. 794 until the Meiji Restoration of 1868, is located two hours and fifty minutes west of Tokyo by Shinkansen (about forty minutes from Osaka by either the Hankyu or Keihan private lines). Kyoto's cultural treasures—including some 2,000 temples, shrines, palaces, and villas—fortuitously escaped the ravages of World War II bombing due to intervention by Western scholars.

Unlike the mazelike "Eastern Capital" of Tokyo, Kyoto is conveniently arranged in a grid of nine main streets running east and west, and intersected by a series of wide avenues and the Kamogawa river. The city has a very efficient bus system, which is connected to all major sights. Taxis, which are readily available, are also a good means of inner-city transportation. Since many of the main attractions are located in clusters, you might choose to travel by taxi to a selected area, and walk between the nearby sights. (The subway and private train lines are limited, and therefore only useful to the tourist for a few selected destinations.) **The Tourist Information Center** (075) 371-5649; closed Saturday afternoon and all day Sunday) is located on the first floor of Kyoto Tower Building in front of Kyoto Station. Here you can get all kinds of free information in English, including easy-to-understand city maps which indicate bus routes and major sights.

Its great cultural heritage notwithstanding, Kyoto is a major city with a flourishing industrial section on its southern outskirts. Kyoto's main shopping and nightlife districts, easily accessible by bus from the terminal in front of

The Golden Pavilion of Kinkaku-ji temple, in Kyoto

Kyoto station, are located near the intersection of Shijodori Avenue and Kawaramachi Boulevard, on both sides of the Kamogawa river. Kawaramachi, Pontocho, and Kiyamachi are on the west side of the river, with the more traditional Gion on the east side. Kawaramachi, Kyoto's version of Ginza, has large department stores, countless modern and traditional specialty shops, restaurants, and pubs. Although the parallel streets of Pontocho and Kiyamachi preserve some of their traditional atmosphere, much of this is now dominated by discos, pubs, cabarets, and restaurants popular with the young.

The very mention of Gion, Kyoto's famous geisha quarter, still conjures up images of white-painted *maiko* (apprentice geisha) entertaining guests at Japanese teahouses. By all means take an evening stroll through Gion's brightly lit back streets, lined with wooden houses of latticed windows and black tile roofs. Although entrance to the exclusive geisha houses requires an introduction, such is not the case with most of the restaurants, where anyone can experience the delicate flavors of authentic Kyoto cuisine.

Suggested Kyoto Sights

The tourist will only be able to take in a small portion of what Kyoto has to offer on any visit. The sights and tastes of Kyoto are best savored unhurriedly. The following are some suggestions.

Sanjusangendo Hall, just a short taxi ride from Kyoto Station, is a convenient starting place. This long "Hall of Thirty-Three Bays" was thus named for the thirty-three spaces between the pillars in front of the main altar. The sight inside the dimly lit hall is spectacular. One thousand gilded wooden Kannon statues, each with eleven faces and numerous arms, form six rows flanking a larger Kannon which stands at the center of the altar. An annual archery tournament is held every January 15 on the rear veranda, a tradition which dates back to the beginning of the Edo period.

Across the street is the **Kyoto National Museum** (open 9:00 A.M.–4:30 P.M.; closed Mondays; admission charge), whose superb collection includes precious art objects and historical treasures from the area's temples and shrines. The brick Meiji-era old wing, built in the French Renaissance style, is in itself a work of art.

Apprentice geishas chatting in the afternoon

From here it is only a short cab ride to one of Kyoto's most famous sights, **Kiyomizu Temple** ("Temple of Pure Water"), located in the wooded Higashiyama hills above the east side of the city. The uphill approach to the temple is lined with shops selling Kiyomizu pottery, paper dolls, Japanese sweets, and other traditional souvenirs. Kiyomizu Temple was founded in A.D. 780, but most of its buildings were rebuilt in 1633. The magnificent Main Hall, built upon a towering scaffold, is a national treasure whose veranda is particularly famous for its panoramic view of the city.

After looking around the expansive grounds of the temple, backtrack down the approach and spend some time exploring the quaint stone-paved streets below. These roads include an architecturally preserved zone lined with old houses, teahouses, and shops selling porcelain, stoneware, and other crafts unique to the area. A leisurely stroll down the inclined Sannenzaka road will bring you near Yasaka Pagoda (erected 1440, repaired 1618). Close by is the vermilion **Yasaka Shrine** which, though located on the eastern edge of the city, represents the heart of Kyoto. Unlike most of Kyoto's other shrines and temples, whose history is closely related to the aristocratic and samurai classes, Yasaka Shrine has traditionally been the domain of the townspeople. Famous as the host of Gion Matsuri, Kyoto's big summer festival, this shrine is visited by hundreds of thousands of pilgrims every New Year's Eve. Its unique temple-like Main Hall, an important cultural property, is noted for its magnificent cypress-shingled roof. **Maruyama Koen**, Kyoto's main public park, is located nearby at the eastern end of Shijodori Avenue at the foot of the hills. The cherry blossoms in April here

Kyoto's stately Heian Shrine

are a sight to behold.

A pleasant stroll at the foot of the Higashiyama hills is along **Philosopher's Way**, a canal-side path whose tranquil atmosphere is conducive to deep contemplation. The three-quarter mile (1.2 kilometers) gravel way, along which you will encounter an occasional temple and imperial tomb, leads through a residential district to another famous Higashiyama sight, **Ginkaku-ji** (Temple of the Silver Pavilion). The eighth Ashikaga Shogun, Yoshimasa, built this temple in 1483 as a retirement villa, but never succeeded in covering its wooden exterior in silver leaf as he had intended. On the grounds of the temple, where the tea ceremony originated, is Japan's oldest tea room.

In the northern Kitayama hills on the other side of Kyoto is **Kinkaku-ji**, built in 1397 by the third Ashikaga Shogun, Yoshimitsu, who did succeed in gilding the temple's Golden Pavilion. The pavilion was burned down in 1950 by a deranged priest, on whom Yukio Mishima based his famous novel *The Golden Pavilion*. The present Golden Pavilion, its walls completely covered in gold foil,

is an exact replica of the original. Its image shimmering in the pond facing it, the structure is enhanced by the beautiful surrounding garden and wooded area.

From here it is only a short cab ride to the lavishly decorated **Nijo Castle**, situated within the moat near the center of the city. Originally built in 1603 as the official Kyoto residence of Tokugawa Ieyasu, the castle served as a symbol of power and authority of the Tokugawa Shogunate. Hour-long tours in English are available throughout the day. The grounds include beautiful gardens, original ramparts, imposing gates, and the ruins of the donjon, but the main attraction is the magnificent Ninomaru Palace. Remove your shoes before entering this national treasure, which consists of five buildings (thirty-three rooms), made almost entirely of Japanese cypress, and designed by the finest craftsmen of the day. Tourists walk freely through dimly lit wooden corridors to view these rooms, many of whose sliding wall dividers consist of elaborate paintings by great artists of the Kano School. There is one section of the corridor called "Nightingale Floor" for the loud birdlike creaking sound it makes when trod upon. This was a kind of alarm system to warn of would-be assassins. Of particular historical significance are the First and Second Grand Chambers, the most important official audience rooms of the palace. Gorgeously adorned in gold and lacquer, these chambers were used by the Tokugawa court to impress visiting lords. It was in the First and Second Grand Chambers that the last Shogun, Tokugawa Yoshinobu, announced his decision in 1867 to restore sovereignty to the Imperial Court. Today, the historic scene is depicted with life-size mannequins dressed in the formal garb of high-ranking samurai.

Nara

*F*ree of the booming modernization of Kyoto, Nara (thirty-three minutes from Kyoto Kintetsu Station on the Kyoto Kintetsu Line, and sixty minutes from Kyoto JR Station by the JR Nara Line) is a rural town of only 330,000, whose idyllic atmosphere complements its ancient culture. Often called the cradle of Japanese civilization, Nara became the nation's first permanent capital in A.D. 710, thus beginning an era of unprecedented development in the fields of art and politics. Although Nara never achieved the elegance that was to be Kyoto's, during its seventy-four years as the Japanese capital Buddhism gained powerful influence over the Imperial Court, magnificent temples were built, and literary and historical classics were written.

Deer graze in Nara Park near Kofuku-ji temple

Nara Sights

The immense **Nara Park**, where deer roam freely, is just a short stroll east of Kintetsu Nara Station, or a fifteen-minute walk from JR Nara Station. Centered around the park are Nara's main sights, the foremost of which is **Todai-ji**, the temple of the **Great Buddha**. The Great Buddha, the world's largest bronze statue, was completed in A.D. 752 by the Emperor Shomu as a symbol of his authority over the Japanese Buddhist state. Both the Great Buddha Hall, which houses the statue, and the Great Buddha itself are national treasures, though neither retains its original appearance. The hall, which was burned down twice, was restored in 1709. Although it has been reduced to one-third of its former size, the Great Buddha Hall is the largest wooden structure in the world.

Todai-ji temple itself was burned twice before being rebuilt in the early seventeenth century. The few original structures and objects which survive today are among Japan's most precious cultural treasures. **Sangatsu-do** (also called *Hokke-do*) hall, built in A.D. 733, is the oldest surviving building of Todai-ji. This small modest hall contains some of the greatest examples of eighth-century Japanese Buddhist sculpture. The nearby **Kaidan-in Ordination Hall** contains the celebrated eighth-century clay images of the Four Deva Kings, staunch defenders of Buddhism.

Two superb museums in the park are the **Nara National Museum** (open 9:00 A.M.–4:30 P.M.; closed Mondays) and the **National Treasure House** (open daily, 9:00 A.M.–5:00 P.M.). The Nara National Museum has a fantastic collection of Buddhist art, mostly from the Asuka, Hakuho, and Nara periods. In its possession are several hundred paintings; many pieces of sculpture, handicrafts, and calligraphy; as well as objects used in Buddhist rites, sutras and sutra boxes, and mandalas. The National Treasure House contains masterpieces from the Nara and Kamakura periods that belong to the nearby Kofuku-ji temple.

Horyu-ji (twelve minutes from JR Nara Station by Kansai main line) is Japan's oldest surviving temple complex and contains the most ancient wooden structures in the world. Horyu-ji was founded in A.D. 607 by Prince Shotoku, who is considered the father of both Japanese Buddhism and the Japanese state. Inside the temple's Kondo, or "Golden Hall," which dates from the seventh century, are several priceless Buddhist statues. The most famous of these is the bronze Shaka Trinity cast in A.D. 623 by Tori Busshi, the earliest artist on record in Japan. The pagoda to the west of the Kondo is Japan's oldest standing pagoda. The nearby Great Treasure Hall houses many of Horyu-ji's treasures. Among these is the wooden Kudara Kannon, a masterpiece of Buddhist sculpture whose origins are obscure.

Yakushi-ji temple creates a mood of serenity

Osaka

Osaka, the business center of the Kansai region in western Japan, is three hours from Tokyo by Shinkansen. Although its population of 2,635,000 makes it the third largest Japanese city (second to Yokohama), the scale of Osaka's industry and commerce is only surpassed by that of Tokyo. In fact, many of Japan's corporations have their headquarters in Osaka, which is the transportation hub of the Kansai region. The city proper encompasses a wide area divided into twenty-six wards, with its main business areas located along the JR Osaka Kanjo (loop) Line. There are three main railway junctions within the city: Umeda, Namba, and Tennoji Stations, all of which are connected by the Midosuji Subway Line (one of Osaka's seven subway lines) to each other and Shin Osaka Station, Osaka's Shinkansen stopping point. While the Shinkansen and domestic airlines connect Osaka to the rest of Japan, Osaka International Airport links the city to the world, and a new international airport, built on reclaimed land in Osaka Bay, is due to be completed in the spring of 1993.

Osaka's modern history began when the powerful warlord Toyotomi Hideyoshi built the country's largest castle here at the end of the sixteenth century. During the Edo period Osaka flourished as the "Kitchen of Japan," serving as a national distribution center for products from the local provinces. A thriving merchant culture developed in this city, which gave birth to the dramatic art form of *bunraku* (puppet theater), and in modern times a unique style of *manzai* (comic stage dialogue).

There are two major shopping and dining areas in Osaka. One is **Kita**, centered around Umeda Station, the traffic nucleus of the city. Often compared to Tokyo's Ginza, Kita has many modern stores, an extensive underground shopping center, cinemas, and theaters, among which is the **National Bunraku Theater** (212-2531; five-minute walk from Kintetsu Nihonbashi Subway Station). Traditional puppet drama is performed here from around 11:00 A.M. to 4:00 P.M., in January, April, June, July, August and November. (English program notes and earphone guides are available.)

Osaka Sights

Osaka Castle, Osaka's greatest sight, is a ten-minute walk from Temmabashi Station on the Tanimachi Subway Line. When Hideyoshi chose Osaka as the site for his mighty castle, he envisioned a commercial center here separate from the intrigue of the imperial capital in Kyoto. It was for this purpose that the warlord persuaded, and in some cases ordered merchants from nearby localities to move here. Osaka subsequently served as the mercantile capital of Japan throughout the Edo period, and it was here that the nation's first mint was built in 1870. Osaka Castle's main attraction is its tremendous concrete donjon, a 1931 reconstruction of the original which was destroyed in 1868. Displayed in the five-tiered donjon are objects related to Hideyoshi, and Osaka history. Cherries bloom in **Nishinomaru Park** to the west of the donjon, while **Osaka Castle Park** to the east is famous for its plum blossoms.

The **Fujita Art Museum** (351-0582; open 10:00 A.M.–4:00 P.M., closed Mondays; admission: ¥700) is a ten-minute walk from Kyobashi Station on the JR loop. Displayed here is Baron Fujita's important Japanese and Chinese art collection, including nine national treasures. The building itself is of an old storehouse which was part of the Fujita estate.

Shitennoji (open 8:30 A.M.–4:00 P.M.),

Osaka Castle, reconstructed after WWII

buildings, a huge underground shopping center, and numerous high-class restaurants, bars, and nightclubs. Osaka's other major entertainment area is **Minami**, situated around Namba Station, near the center of the JR loop. Minami's bustling Namba district is particularly popular for its traditional, down-to-earth atmosphere which retains Osaka's mercantile past. Inexpensive but good restaurants and pubs are numerous here. Among the district's most famous restaurants is **Kanidoraku** (567-0051), located in Dotonbori on the south bank of the canal. The giant mechanical crab above the entrance is indicative of the variety of crab dishes served here. Minami also has department the birthplace of Japanese Buddhism and one of Japan's oldest temples, is a five-minute walk from Shitennoji-mae Station on both the JR loop and Midosuji Subway Line. The famed Prince Shotoku built the original in A.D. 593, dedicating the temple to Buddhism's Four Heavenly Guardians (Shitenno) for their help in defeating his anti-Buddhist rivals. The nearby **Tennoji Park** contains a Botanic Garden (open 9:30 A.M.–5:00 P.M.), Tennoji zoo (open 9:30 A.M.–5:00 P.M.) and the serene Keitakuen Garden (open Tuesdays, Thursdays, and Sundays 9:30 A.M.–4:30 P.M.), all closed Mondays.

Near Yodoyabashi Station is **Nakanoshima**, an island in the river with imposing Western buildings and bridges. Among these is Nakanoshima Library (built 1904), located in Nakanoshima Park. The library's entrance hall is an important cultural property modeled after the Pantheon. Nearby is the **Osaka Museum of Oriental Ceramics** (223-0055; open 9:30 A.M.–5:00 P.M.; closed Mondays and the day after a holiday; admission: ¥500), whose small but distinguished collection of Japanese, Chinese, and Korean pottery is exhibited with natural lighting.

Kanidoraku provides one of Osaka's landmarks

Sapporo

Sapporo, the capital of Japan's northernmost island of Hokkaido, is one hour and twenty-five minutes by air from Tokyo's Haneda Airport. (Hokkaido's Chitose Airport is twenty-eight minutes from Sapporo Station by express on the JR Chitose Line.) Since most of Hokkaido was developed only over the past century, its greatest cultural and historical aspects have to do with the island's aboriginal Ainu people, and the relics of its frontier days. But perhaps the greatest lure of this sparsely populated island is the great outdoors. There are breath-taking national parks; an abundance of hot springs resulting from the volcanic terrain; peaceful, idyllic dairy farms; corn and potato fields, and some of Japan's best ski slopes.

Sapporo, with a population of 1,528,000, is the fifth largest city in Japan, and the largest city north of Tokyo. Its attractive streets form a grid which is easily traveled on foot, although the subway and taxis are also efficient means of getting around, particularly in the dead of winter. Since hosting the 1972 winter Olympics, Sapporo has taken on a contemporary look, with new Western-style hotels, a Tokyo-like business district near Sapporo Station, big-name department stores, and a large underground shopping arcade near Odori Park, the center of town. Susukino, located in the south of the city, has become one of Japan's hottest nightlife districts outside of Tokyo. But there are still late-nineteenth-century Victorian frame buildings surviving throughout, adding charm to the city.

Sapporo Sights

Most of Sapporo's sights are within walking distance from each other, in close proximity to Sapporo Station in the northern part of the city. The red-brick

Sapporo's Clock Tower rings in the New Year

Old Hokkaido Government Building (open 9:00 A.M.–5:00 P.M.; closed Saturdays, Sundays, and national holidays), a symbol of Sapporo, is a magnificent neo-Baroque monument from the Meiji era. Inside is a reconstruction of the old governor's office, and a small museum which focuses on local history.

Just west of here are the expansive **Botanical Gardens** (open 9:00 A.M.–4:00 P.M., closed Mondays and in the winter), with some 4,500 different plants from all over the world, including flowers in season from April to November. The Gardens' **Bachelor Museum**, specializing in Ainu culture, exhibits tools, weapons, costumes, basketwork, ritual implements, textiles, and other objects of the Ainu.

The white wooden **Clock Tower Building** (open 9:00 A.M.–4:00 P.M.; closed Mondays and the day after a national holiday), located towards the center of the city, is another Meiji-era monument and symbol of Sapporo. The giant clock on top of the building has rung every day at noon since it was constructed in 1881. Inside is a museum dedicated to Sapporo's history.

Odori Park, the city's "green belt" along the center of Odori Boulevard, is the site of the world-famous Sapporo Snow Festival in early February. Snow brought in from the mountains nearby are transformed into enormous, entertaining snow sculptures. At the eastern end of the park is Sapporo TV Tower (open daily 9:30 A.M.–8:30 P.M.; admission: ¥600) which offers a panoramic view of the city.

Sapporo Beer Brewery, established in 1876, was Japan's first brewery. Guided tours (in Japanese only) are available daily at regular intervals between 9:00 A.M. and 3:30 P.M. The old red-brick factory building has been converted into a beer hall (open daily 11:30 A.M.–9:00 P.M.), where a meal of Mongolian barbecue, seafood stew, and draft beer costs ¥2,700 for all you can eat and drink in two hours.

Odori Park, the site of Sapporo's famous Snow Festival

Fukuoka

Fukuoka (population 1,200,000) is the largest city on the island of Kyushu, and the cultural, education, political, business and transportation hub of southern Japan. Located in northern Kyushu, Fukuoka's **Hakata Station** is the terminus of the 723-mile-long Tokaido-Sanyo *shinkansen* bullet train which originates in Tokyo. The trip from Tokyo by *shinkansen* takes six hours and forty minutes, but just one hour and forty minutes by air.

Until the Meiji era the city was divided into two sections. Fukuoka, to the west of the Nakagawa river, was the samurai enclave and site of **Fukuoka Castle**. East of the Nakagawa was **Hakata**, a district set aside entirely for merchants and craftsmen. Although today the whole town is officially called Fukuoka, Hakata (and the nearby Tenjin district) is the bustling commercial center and the name by which most of the local people prefer to call their city, while Fukuoka is the chic business and entertainment district.

Fukuoka has two municipal subway lines. The No. 1 subway line links Hakata Station to Nakasu Kawabata, one of Japan's more popular nightlife districts, and also passes through Fukuoka's main shopping area around Tenjin Station.

Fukuoka Sights

All that remain of Fukuoka Castle are a reconstructed gate and turret, but a panoramic view of the city is afforded from the hill where the mighty citadel once stood. Northwest of the castle grounds is **Ohori Park**, which was built from the outer moat. The park contains a huge pond with an islet at the center, which is accessible by several bridges.

Shofuku-ji, a short walk from the Gion subway stop, was established in 1195 as the first center of Zen teachings in Japan.

Dazaifu Tenmangu, a famous temple in Fukuoka

Shofuku-ji's grounds are where Japan's first tea is believed to have been planted.

Nearby is Fukuoka's most important shrine, **Kushida Jinja**, dedicated to the Shinto god Susano-o-no-Mikoto. The rousing Gion Yamagasa festival is held here every July 1-15. On the final day teams of men race through town carrying huge, colorful floats (at other times the floats are exhibited in the museum attached to the shrine). Another shrine worth visiting in Fukuoka is the **Dazaifu Tenmangu**, which memorializes the revered scholar-statesman Sugawara Michizane.

The **Fukuoka City Museum** (092-714-6051; near Nishizaki subway stop; open 9:30 A.M.–5:00 P.M.; closed Mondays; admission: ¥200) includes exhibits of medieval Japan and various historical scenes and personages, showing people's lifestyle in the middle ages, warlord Toyotomi Hideyoshi's restoration of Fukuoka, the defense of Nagasaki by Fukuoka samurai, and Hakata in the Meiji era.

History buffs may also enjoy the **Mongol Invasion Memorial Hall** (near the Chiyo Kencho-guchi subway stop; open daily 10:00 A.M.–4:00 P.M.; admission: ¥300) in Higashi Park. Exhibits include a Mongol helmet, armor, and weapons which were used during the Mongol invasion of Japan in the thirteenth century.

Nagoya

Nagoya, Japan's fourth largest city, is two hours from Tokyo Station by Shinkansen or one hour by air from Narita. The city serves as a gateway to central Japan, which includes such major resort areas as Ise-Shima National Park and the Japan Alps, and Nagoya Port is one of the largest international harbors in Japan. Domestic airlines such as ANA fly out of Nagoya Airport to major destinations all over the country, as well as to some international destinations. Bus service, available from Nagoya airport to the inner city, takes about forty minutes.

Most of Nagoya's historical and cultural monuments were unfortunately destroyed by World War II bombing, which subsequently led to Nagoya's reconstruction as a modern city.

Today four subway lines provide pub-

Atsuta Jingu shrine

lic transportation throughout Nagoya, and all signs at the subway stations are written in both Japanese and English. Nagoya's downtown area and main entertainment district is **Sakae**, located about 1.5 miles (2.5 kilometers) from Nagoya Station. The city's 590 foot (180 meter) tall TV Tower is in Sakae, as is the beautiful **Hisaya Odori Park**. Another bustling center is the area around Nagoya Station.

Nagoya Castle

Nagoya Sights

Nagoya Castle (052-231-1700; open 9:00 A.M.–4:30 P.M.; closed New Year's holidays; admission: ¥500) is a five-minute walk from Shiyakusho Station on the Meijo Subway Line. The original castle, one of the greatest fortresses in Japan, was completed in 1614. It was destroyed during World War II, and all that remains of the original are three turrets, one gate, and the stone foundations. The concrete reconstruction contains beautiful screens which were salvaged from the original castle, and on the grounds is a replica of a tea arbor buit by Oda Nobunaga. Nagoya Castle is symbolized by the reconstructed golden dolphins atop the roof of the donjon, placed there to guard against fire. From the observatory on top of the donjon is an expansive view of the city of Nagoya and the Nobi Plain.

The **Tokugawa Art Museum** (935-6262; open 10:00 A.M.–5:00 P.M.; closed Mondays and New Year's holidays; admission: ¥1,000) is a ten-minute walk from Ozone Station on the Meijo Subway Line, the JR Chuo Line, or the Meitetsu Seto Line. Built on the grounds of a former mansion of the Lord of Owari, the museum houses some 11,000 treasures—swords, armor, paintings, pottery, lacquer ware and other works of art—including the exquisite picture scroll illustrating scenes from *The Tale of Genji*, and seven other national treasures. (The *Genji* scroll, however, is only displayed once a year.)

Atsuta Jingu shrine, accessible by the Meijo Subway Line, the JR Tokaido Line, or the Meitetsu Tokoname Line, is the second most important shrine after Ise. Housed here is the imperial sword, one of three sacred symbols of the Japanese emperor.

Useful Telephone Numbers

Selected Embassies and Consulates

Argentina	5420-7101
Australia	5232-4111
Austria	3451-8281
Belgium	3262-0191
Brazil	3404-5211
Bulgaria	3465-1021
Canada	3408-2101
Chile	3452-7561
Czech/Slovak Republic	3400-8122
Denmark	3496-3001
Finland	3442-2231
France	3473-0171
Germany	3473-0151
Greece	3403-0871
Hungary	3798-8801
Italy	3453-5291
Netherlands	5401-0411
New Zealand	3467-2271
Norway	3440-2611
Peru	3406-4240
Poland	3711-5224
Portugal	3400-7907
Romania	3479-0311
Russian Federation	3583-4224
South Africa	3265-3366
Spain	3583-8531
Sweden	5562-5050
Switzerland	3473-0121
United Kingdom	3265-5511
United States of America	3224-5000
Yugoslavia	3447-3571

Transportation Offices
- Haneda Airport Information 5747-8111
- Immigration Information Center (Otemachi) 3213-8523
- Narita Flight Information (0476)34-5000
- Airport Limousine Bus Service Center 3665-7220
- Shinkansen (JR East Infoline) 3423-0111
- Keisei Skyliner (Ueno–Narita) 3831-2528
- Tokyo City Air Terminal (TCAT) 3665-7111

Miscellaneous
- American Pharmacy (English spoken) 3271-4034
- International Telegram 3344-5151
- International Telephone Operator 0051
- Japan Helpline (toll-free) 0120-46-1997
- Japan Hotline 3586-0110
- Lost and found:
  Police (in Japanese) 3814-4151
  Taxi (in Japanese) 3648-0300
  EIDAN Subway (in Japanese) 3834-5577
  Metropolitan Buses and Subways (in Japanese) 5600-2020
  Japan Railways 3423-0111
- Metropolitan Police Department (in English) 3581-4321
- Telephone Directory Service (in English) 3851-1621
- Tokyo Central Post Office 3284-9537
- Tokyo English Life Line (TELL) 5721-4347
- Tokyo International Post Office 3241-4839

Tokyo Calendar

The dates to the following sampling of main events and festivals may change according to the lunar calendar. It's best to confirm by checking with an English-language press or by calling Tourist Information Center at 3502-1461. (See also National Holidays)

January 1–3: Hatsumode.

The year's first visit to a shrine or temple to pray for happiness for the coming year. Sensoji temple, Meiji Shrine, and Zojoji temple are popular. On the second, the Imperial Palace grounds are open to the public.

January 8: Dondo-yaki.

New Year decorations are burned in a bonfire, after which pounded rice cakes (o-mochi) are toasted in the embers to bring health and good fortune during the year. (Torigoe Shrine in Taito ward.)

February 3 or 4: Setsubun.

Bean throwing festival to drive out bad luck and bring in good fortune. This marks the beginning of the new year, according to the lunar calendar. (Zojoji temple, Sensoji temple, Torigoe Shrine, etc.)

Early to Mid-February: Tako Ichi.

Many types of kites are on sale at Oji Inari Shrine in Kita ward, which are said to be charms against fire.

February 15–March 14: Ume Matsuri.

Festival of plum blossoms. (Yushima Shrine in Bunkyo ward).

March 3: Hina Matsuri.

Doll Festival, also called Girls' Day, wishes happiness and prosperity for the girls in the family. Dolls in elegant, ancient costumes are displayed in homes.

March 3 and 4: Daruma Ichi.

Jindaiji temple festival with red daruma dolls on sale. These dolls bring good fortune when one of its eyes is painted in. A promise is made to paint the other eye when the wish is granted.

Early April: O-hanami.

A celebration of cherry blossom viewing throughout the city, including Chidorigafuchi, Ueno Park, Aoyama Cemetery, and Sumida Park.

May 5: Boys' Festival.

Warrior dolls and carp streamers are displayed at homes to wish for good health for the boys in the family.

Mid-May: Kanda Matsuri.

Held in odd-numbered years, one of the three large festivals held by the Edo people. Portable shrines (o-mikoshi), are paraded from Kanda Shrine through the streets of Otemachi and Nihonbashi.

Third Thursday–Sunday in May: Sanja Matsuri.

Another of the big Edo festivals, this one held at Asakusa Shrine.

May 31–June 1: Potted Plant Fair.

Held at Sengen Shrine, a branch of one on the summit of Mt. Fuji, to herald the opening of the mountain to the public.

First or second Sunday in June: Torigoe Festival.

An after-dark lantern-lit procession with a four-ton portable shrine borne by 200 men. (Torigoe Shrine in Taito ward.)

June 10–16: Sanno Matsuri.

Another Edo-period parade held in even-numbered years (alternating with Kanda Matsuri). An ox-drawn sacred palanquin, along with mounted shrine officials wind their way around the imperial palace and through the streets of Ginza and Kyobashi. (Hie Shrine in Akasaka.)

July 6–8: Morning Glory Fair.

Begun in early Meiji period, over 100 stalls are set up before dawn to sell morning glory plants. (Iriya Kishimojin in Taito ward.)

July 9–10: Hozuki Fair.

Begun in the middle of the Edo period. The ground cherry is traditionally believed to cure children of tantrums. Besides potted plants, traditional shitamachi crafts connected with ground cherries are also on sale. (Sensoji temple in Asakusa.)

Late July: Sumida River Fireworks.

Carried over from Edo times when the river was "opened" for summer pleasure boats by purging it of cholera's evil spirits. Since 1982, a fireworks competition has made the displays even more spectacular.

Second weekend in August: Tsukuda Festival.

Bon dance held at Sumiyoshi Shrine at Tsukudajima, since 1580.

Early to Mid-August: Takigi Noh.

Noh performances are held by torchlight at Hie Shrine in Akasaka.

The annual Sumida River Fireworks display in July

Parading portable shrines during the Kanda Festival

Daruma dolls on sale at Jindai-ji temple

Mid-August to Late September.

After O-Bon (a Buddhist holiday during which ancestral spirits are believed to return), usually mid-August in Tokyo, many local shrine festivals are held throughout the city.

September 25: Ningyo Kuyo.

Childless couples offer dolls to the Kannon goddess of mercy and pray for fertility. At Kiyomizu Temple in Ueno Park, dolls are burned accompanied by the chanting of sutras.

October 11–13: O-eshiki.

Nighttime lantern procéssion to commemorate the death of Buddhist priest Nichiren in 1282. (Ikegami Honmonji temple in Ota ward.)

Several days in November: Tori no Ichi.

Held on Days of the Cock according to the zodiac calendar. Tradespeople and shopkeepers flock to several Otori shrines in Tokyo to pray for business prosperity, many buying bamboo rakes with good-luck charms.

November 15: Shichigosan.

Girls aged three and seven, and boys of five are taken by their parents to Shinto shrines, dressed up in their holiday best, to give thanks for safe growth and to pray for future blessings. (Meiji Shrine, Hie Shrine, Asakusa Shrine, etc.)

December 14: Gishi-sai.

Festival celebrating the loyalty of the famous 47 ronin (Lord Asano's samurai vassals) on the revenge of their master's death. (Sengakuji temple in Minato ward.)

December 15–16: Boro Ichi.

A 400-year old fair begun by the lord of Odawara for the local people. About 700 stalls selling all kinds of household goods, antiques, plants, and clothes, etc. are set up along the Tokyu Setagaya Line between Setagaya and Kamimachi Stations.

December 31–January 1: Joya no Kane.

Bells begin tolling around midnight at Buddhist temples throughout Japan to clear away evil human passions. Japanese visit shrines and temples to pray for health, happiness, and prosperity in the new year, after which soba, symbolizing health and long life, is traditionally eaten.

All Nippon Airways

Dedication to service has made All Nippon Airways one of the largest airlines in the world in less than forty years. In addition to boasting the greatest domestic air capacity in Japan (518 daily flights to 96 cities, as of June 1996), ANA flies to twenty cities in eighteen other countries (as of June 1996), including New York, Los Angeles, Washington, D.C., London, Moscow, Vienna, Beijing, Seoul, Bangkok, Singapore, Hong Kong, Sydney, Paris, Frankfurt, and Shanghai, etc.

ANA's First Class passengers get nothing but the very best: separate check-in counters; an exclusive lounge for a quiet, relaxing rest before departure; priority boarding, de-planing and baggage handling; luxurious free-reclining seats with ample room to stretch out that are placed a spacious 82 inches apart; and that recline fully to 180 degrees (on U.S. and European flights); and, of course, the finest service throughout the flight, including five-star cuisine, wines, cocktails, and other beverages.

ANA's business class "CLUB ANA" is designed to make business travel smooth and comfortable. Quality service includes access to a plush business lounge before boarding; priority check-in and baggage handling; a spacious seat pitch of 50 inches (most trans-Pacific and European routes); TV set and CD audio equipment in all seats (some aircraft); bilingual cabin attendants; and international cuisines carefully prepared from market-fresh ingredients, complemented with fine wines, cocktails, and other beverages.

Nor does ANA's dedication to service end after you have landed. Complimentary limousine service awaits all First Class and CLUB ANA passengers arriving at Beijing and London. This includes chauffeur-driven cars to Beijing hotels; and limousine cars between Heathrow Airport to any area within a radius of 40 miles. (Reservations are needed 48 hours before departure.) There is also the Sky Porter service for luggage handling from the airport to one's home, office, hotel, or other destination, after de-boarding. (Those desiring Sky Porter service should call any ANA ticket agency three days in advance.)

A network of forty ANA hotels includes the luxurious ANA Hotel in Tokyo, the superb new ANA Hotel Narita, near the New Tokyo International Airport, ANA Hotel San Francisco, ANA Hotel Washington, D.C., Delta Grand Pacific Hotel, Bangkok, Beijing New Century Hotel, ANA Grand Castle Hotel Xian, Century Park Hotel, Manila, ANA Hotel Sydney, ANA Grand Hotel Wien, Pacific Star Hotel in Guam, and a growing international network in business and resort locations around the Pacific.

The ANA CARD, issued in conjunction with either Visa, Master, or JCB cards, is a multipurpose credit card for the world traveler. Use the ANA CARD for all of your traveling needs, including airline tickets, hotels, car rentals, foreign exchange, international telephone service (in Japan), and the ANA Sky Shop (on board only), as well as for general use. Additional information is available at ANA ticket offices in cities throughout the world. The ANA CARD can only be used by residents in Japan.

In addition, the new international mileage service, called Program A, lets you earn mileage coupons by flying on ANA and eight other airlines, as well as by staying at any ANA hotel outside Japan. This worldwide network offers you international flight and upgrade coupons.

ANA HOTELS

ANA Hotels Toll-Free USA/CANADA 800-ANA-HOTELS
Tokyo Reservation Center Tel (03) 3505-1181 Fax (03) 3505-1180
ANA Hotels Sales Offices (Japan): **Sapporo** Tel (011) 232-2011 Fax (011) 232-2020
Nagoya Tel (052) 971-0789 Fax (052) 951-6457 **Osaka** Tel (06) 374-1661 Fax (06)
375-4593 **Fukuoka** Tel (092) 411-2111 Fax (092) 474-7370 **Pacific Star Hotel Tokyo
Sales Office** Tel (03) 3505-1170 Fax (03) 3505-1152 **Los Angeles** Tel (213) 955-7677
Fax (213) 955-7678 **New York** Tel (212) 332-1500 Fax (212) 582-0300 **Chicago** Tel
(312) 553-9191 Fax (312) 553-9192 **London** Tel (171) 493-4856 Fax (171) 493-5577
Hong Kong Tel 2845 4280 Fax 2845 5106 **Singapore** Tel 734-0835 Fax 733-2401

ANA Hotel Tokyo	(03) 3505-1111
ANA Hotel Narita	(0476) 33-1311
ANA Hotel Kyoto	(075) 231-1155
ANA Hotel Osaka	(06) 347-1112
ANA Hotel Sapporo	(011) 221-4411
ANA Hotel Kushiro	(0154) 31-4111
ANA Hotel Wakkanai	(0162) 23-8111
ANA Hotel Kanazawa	(0762) 24-6111
ANA Hotel Hiroshima	(082) 241-1111
ANA Hotel Ube	(0836) 32-1112
ANA Hotel Matsuyama	(089) 933-5511
ANA Hotel Hakata	(092) 471-7111
ANA Hotel JR Huis Ten Bosch	(0956) 58-7111
Hakodate Harborview Hotel	(0138) 22-0111
Hotel Castle (Yamagata)	(0236) 31-3311
Bandai Silver Hotel (Niigata)	(025) 243-3711
ANA Hotel Passtel Kyoto	(075) 213-0111
Takamatsu Grand Hotel	(0878) 51-5757
Fukuoka Hotel Umino-nakamichi	(092) 603-2525
New Sky Hotel (Kumamoto)	(096) 354-2111
Hirado Kanko Hotel Ranpu	(0950) 23-2111
Yoronto Kanko Hotel	(0997) 97-2551
Okinawa Harborview Hotel	(098) 853-2111
Okinawa Oceanview Hotel	(098) 853-2112
Palace on the Hill Okinawa	(098) 864-1111
Laguna Garden Hotel (Okinawa)	(098) 897-2121
Manza Beach Hotel (Okinawa)	(098) 966-1211
Kumejima Eef Beach Hotel (Okinawa)	(098) 985-7111
Ishigaki Hotel Sun Coast (Okinawa)	(09808) 2-6171
Century Park Hotel (Manila)	63-2 522-1011
ANA Hotel Singapore	65-732-1222
Beijing New Century Hotel	86-10-849-2001
ANA Grand Castle Hotel Xian	86-29-723-1800
Pacific Star Hotel (Guam)	671-649-7827
ANA Hotel Gold Coast (Australia)	61-75-579-1000
ANA Hotel Sydney	61-2-250-6000
ANA Hotel San Francisco	1-415-974-6400
ANA Hotel Washington D.C.	1-202-429-2400
ANA Grand Hotel Wien	43-1-515800

ANA Gate Tower Hotel Osaka (to open Oct. '96)
ANA Hotel Chitose (to open May '97)

ANA Reservations in Japan

For International Flights

Free Dial Service	0120-029-333
Tokyo	(03) 3272-1212
Osaka	(06) 372-1212
Sapporo	(011) 281-1212
Nagoya	(052) 971-5588
Fukuoka	(092) 474-1212
Okinawa	(098) 861-1212
Kushiro	(0154) 25-0814
Kitami	(0157) 61-3776
Hakodate	(0138) 263525
Sendai	(022) 265-2248
Koriyama	(0249) 21-1111
Akita	(0188) 33-1973
Yamagata	(0236) 32-0779
Shonai	(0235) 25-5575
Kanazawa	(0762) 31-3115
Niigata	(025) 244-5813
Toyama	(0764) 32-3643
Fukui	(0776) 23-6877
Nagano	(026) 235-0312
Yakohama	(045) 663-2562
Chiba	(043) 221-2600
Omiya	(048) 649-1212
Shizuoka	(054) 252-4721
Kyoto	(075) 222-0350
Kobe	(078) 321-6880
Takamatsu	(0878) 25-0135
Kochi	(0888) 82-6136
Matsuyama	(089) 948-3132
Tottori	(0857) 24-0404
Yonago	(0859) 35-0712
Okayama	(086) 224-3109
Hiroshima	(082) 246-0211
Ube	(0836) 33-1221
Kitakyushu	(093) 541-6868
Oita	(0975) 37-2802
Nagasaki	(0958) 22-5115
Kumamoto	(096) 325-0633
Miyazaki	(0985) 26-8101
Kagoshima	(099) 223-2692

For Domestic Flights

Free Dial Service	0120-029-222
Tokyo	(03) 5489-8800
Osaka	(06) 534-8800
Sapporo	(011) 726-8800
Nagoya	(052) 962-6211
Fukuoka	(092) 752-8800
Okinawa	(098) 866-5111

Akita	(0188) 33-1470
Abashiri	(0152) 43-8800
Amamioshima	(0997) 52-7272
Aomori	(0177) 35-1725
Asahikawa	(0166) 23-6261
Beppu	(0977) 21-5111
Chiba	(043) 224-2061
Fukue	(0959) 72-5151
Fukui	(0776) 23-6454
Fukushima	(0245) 21-8800
Gifu	(058) 266-7331
Hachiojima	(04996) 2-1171
Hachioji	(0426) 44-8833
Hakodate	(0138) 26-3521
Hamada	(0855) 22-3400
Hiroshima	(082) 243-2231
Iki	(09204) 7-6633
Kagoshima	(099) 223-2351
Kanazawa	(0762) 31-3111
Kitami	(0157) 61-8800
Kitakyushu	(093) 511-6363
Kobe	(078) 321-3831
Kochi	(0888) 82-6171
Kofu	(0552) 22-2751
Koriyama	(0249) 33-8800
Komatsu	(0761) 24-5211
Kumamoto	(096) 325-1161
Kurume	(0942) 32-2211
Kushiro	(0154) 25-0811
Kyoto	(075) 211-5471
Maebashi	(0272) 23-5101
Masuda(Iwami)	(0856) 23-7733
Matsue	(0852) 31-2080
Matsuyama	(089) 948-3131
Mito	(029) 225-2757
Miyakonojo	(0986) 23-5181
Miyazaki	(0985) 23-5101
Monbetsu	(01582) 3-3100
Morioka	(0196) 25-2431
Muroran	(0143) 47-8800
Nagano	(026) 225-0311
Nagasaki	(0958) 22-5111
Nakashibetsu	(01537) 2-4586
Nankishirahama	(0739) 43-1600
Nara	(0742) 45-1131
Niigata	(025) 244-5812
Obihiro	(0155) 22-6021
Oita	(0975) 37-2800
Okayama	(086) 224-3131
Okushiri	(01397) 3-2301

Omiya	(048) 644-1301	Tokushima	(0886) 25-8800
Omura	(0957) 54-3200	Tomakomai	(0144) 32-8241
Oshima	(04992) 2-2336	Tottori	(0857) 23-3038
Otaru	(0134) 24-1505	Toyama	(0764) 32-2233
Otsu	(0775) 21-0181	Tsu	(0592) 24-5851
Rebun	(01638) 7-2175	Tsuruoka	(0235) 25-8010
Rishiri	(01638) 2-1770	Tsushima	(09205) 2-7171
Saga	(0952) 29-2515	Ube	(0836) 33-1221
Sakata	(0234) 24-8010	Utsunomiya	(028) 663-3941
Sasebo	(0956) 23-6191	Wakayama	(0734) 53-8211
Sakai	(0722) 28-8877	Wakkanai	(0162) 24-2351
Sendai	(022) 265-2244	Yamagata	(0236) 32-0702
Shimonoseki	(0832) 34-1211	Yamaguchi	(0839) 25-1230
Shizuoka	(054) 252-9134	Yokohama	(045) 451-8800
Takamatsu	(0878) 25-0111	Yonago	(0859) 35-0711

ANA International Reservations

USA toll-free number areas (50 States, Canada, Mexico, Puerto Rico, Virgin Islands, but not Guam)   1-800-235-9262

(Japanese)	1-800-262-2230
Other areas in USA	310-782-3011
(Japanese)	310-782-3022
Vancouver	604-303-3636
London	(0171) 355-1155
(Japanese)	(0171) 355-1177
France (toll free number)	(0590) 86-51
(Japanese)	(0590) 86-53
Germany (toll free number)	(0130) 81-6280
(Japanese)	(0130) 81-6282
Austria (toll free number)	(0660) 6717
(Japanese)	(0660) 6757
Belgium (toll free number)	(0800) 1-1381
(Japanese)	(0800) 1-1383
Sweden (toll free number)	(020) 79-2935
(Japanese)	(020) 79-2937
Italy (toll free number)	1678-73671
Holland (toll free number)	06-0229857
Switzerland (toll free number)	155-6369
Spain (toll free number)	900-97-4491
Moscow	(095) 956-4634
Seoul	(02) 752-5500
Beijing	(010) 6505-3311
Dalian	(0411) 263-9744
Qingdao	(0532) 386-9726
Shanghai	(021) 6279-7000
Hong Kong	(2810) 7100
Bangkok	(02) 238-5121
Kuala Lumpur	(03) 202-1331
Singapore	228-3222
Yangon	(01) 248901
Guam	646-9057
Australia (toll free number, except Sydney)	1800-251-6711
Sydney	(02) 367-6711

ANA International Network

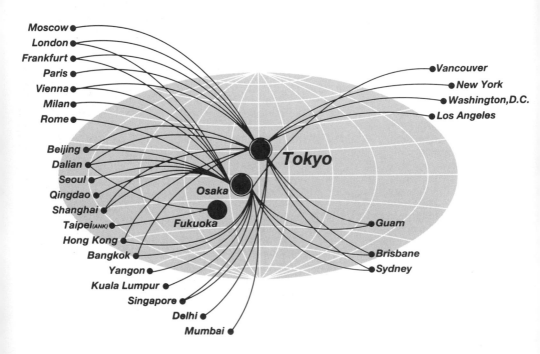

ANA Domestic Network

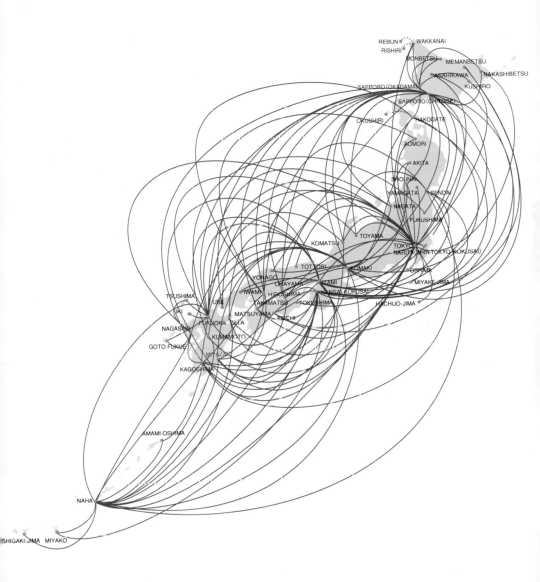

AIRCRAFT INTERIOR LAYOUT

B747-400 テクノジャンボ

● 全長 Length／70.67m　● 翼幅 Wingspan／64.44m　● 全高 Height／19.4m　● 最大離陸重量 Maximum takeoff weight／394,600kg
● 巡航速度 Cruising speed／Mach 0.85　● 航続距離 Range with full load／12,370km

336 seats

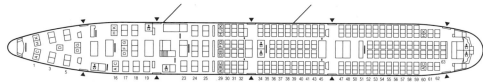

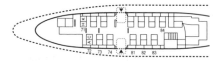

B747-200 スーパージャンボ

● 全長 Length／70.5m　● 翼幅 Wingspan／59.6m　● 全高 Height／19.3m　● 最大離陸重量 Maximum takeoff weight／377,800kg
● 巡航速度 Cruising speed／Mach 0.83　● 航続距離 Range with full load／12,000km

310 seats

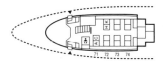

B767-300ER

●全長 Length／54.94m ●翼幅 Wingspan／47.57m ●全高 Height／15.85m ●最大離陸重量 Maximum takeoff weight／156,500kg
●巡航速度 Cruising speed／Mach 0.80 ●航続距離 Range with full load／11,000km

204 seats

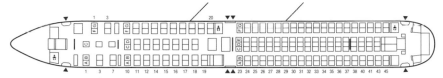

FOR YOUR SAFETY

Your attention to the requests of our cabin attendants and to the following regulations will be greatly appreciated:

• Seat Belts
Please remain seated while the seat-belt sign is illuminated. Also, it is strongly recommended that you keep your seat belt fastened whenever you are seated, as not all turbulence is predictable.

• Smoking Regulations
Please do not smoke in the aisles, lavatories, or in designated no-smoking sections. Also please refrain from smoking cigars and pipes.

• Restrictions on Onboard Use of Electric and Electronic Devices
• Devices that may not be used at any time: FM radios, cellular telephones, transceivers, TVs, pocket pagers, remote-controlled devices, printers, etc.
• Devices that may not be used during takeoff or landing: AM radios, CD players, electronic game devices, video cameras, calculators, electronic diaries, personal computers, word processors, electric shavers, cassette tape recorders, etc.
• Devices that can be used at all times: watches, cameras, battery-operated medical devices (hearing aids, electronic thermometers, pacemakers, etc.)

Standard configuration. Subject to change without notice.

Index

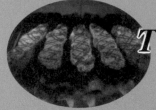